MALS

OF

GRAND CANYON

DONALD F. HOFFMEISTER

ILLUSTRATED BY

JAMES GORDON IRVING

UNIVERSITY OF ILLINOIS PRESS

Urbana   Chicago   London

Photographs on pp. 17, 23, and 27 are reproduced by courtesy of the
Department of the Interior, Grand Canyon National Park. Those on
pp. 20, 21, and 25 are reproduced by courtesy of John Merkle,
Genesee Community College, Flint, Michigan. The photograph on
p. 18 is reproduced by courtesy of Steven W. Carothers, Museum of
Northern Arizona, Flagstaff.

To the Colorado River, sculptress
of the Grand Canyon, and
to John Wesley Powell, her
first scientific explorer

PREFACE

A little over a century ago John Wesley Powell explored the Grand Canyon by way of the Colorado River on a history-making voyage. Even in those early days the University of Illinois, known then as Illinois Industrial University, was sufficiently interested in western exploration that it hired Major Powell as professor of natural history, specifically to conduct this expedition as the university's representative. As we begin the second century of canyon exploration, it is appropriate that this university's interest in field work and research in the Grand Canyon be dedicated to John Wesley Powell and be published by its own press.

Tens of thousands of written pages and millions of photographs have described the grandeur of Grand Canyon since Major Powell traversed the mighty Colorado. The pages of this book make no attempt to duplicate these efforts but are concerned with the lives and whereabouts of the mammals, other than man, within Grand Canyon National Park. To obtain this information, field work was conducted by personnel from the Museum of Natural History of the University of Illinois during several years, in summer and in winter. In addition, many other sources have provided information about mammals and have made specimens available.

From the University of Illinois, special appreciation is due the following collectors: Wayne H. Davis, Lois Goodpaster, Woodrow W. Goodpaster, Helen E. Hoffmeister, J. Ronald Hoffmeister, Robert G. Hoffmeister, Francis Kruidenier, William Z. Lidicker, Jr., Charles McLaughlin, and Kenneth Nelson.

Other persons who have made important collections in Grand Canyon are, for the United States Biological Surveys, Vernon Bailey, Edward Goldman, and C. Hart Merriam; for the American Museum, Harold Anthony; for the Museum of Northern Arizona, Steven Carothers and George Ruffner.

Various employees of the National Park Service in Grand Canyon have preserved mammal specimens and kept most valuable notes and records. Edwin D. McKee and Louis Shellbach were instrumental in the development of these collections.

James Gordon Irving has captured the mammals of the park in his excellent drawings which are not only artistic but accurate. Mr. Irving is one of our foremost nature-artists, and we appreciate the time he has taken in preparing these illustrations.

All administrators, naturalists, and rangers of Grand Canyon have been most helpful in our work. All cannot be listed, but I would like to thank them all, including the late Harold C. Bryant, who, while superintendent of the park, asked me to make this study and prepare this book, Preston P. Patraw, Robert R. Lovegren, Merrill D. Beal, David Ochsner, Larry Henderson, Peter Bennett, Louise Hinchliffe, Neal G. Guse, Jr., Peter Schuft, and Clyde A. Maxey. In addition, Joseph Hall of San Francisco State University has been most helpful.

The University of Illinois has been most generous in providing funds for field work and research on the mammals of Grand Canyon and throughout the Southwest.

CONTENTS

9

INTRODUCTION

The Grand Canyon is an indescribable wonder of abysses and canyons, of canyons within canyons and gorges within gorges, of colors changing from hour to hour and season to season, of a mighty stream constantly cutting more canyon by its eroding and abrasive actions, of hot deserts and cool damp forests. Great precipitous walls of limestone, sandstone, and granite provide an array of colors that are continuously altered by shadows, clouds, rain, or moonlight. Places with winter snow reaching depths of 30 feet are only a few miles from places of no snow. But these are only small parts of this complex canyon. There is also a living community of animals and plants within the canyon, an interesting community indeed. The great variation in topography and in climatic conditions, the isolation of the North from the South Rim, and the isolation of the buttes within the canyon make the biota all the more interesting.

Furred animals — mammals — live in every part of the canyon, from the Colorado River up the sides of the canyon walls to the tops of the rims. They are present on the buttes and within the side canyons (and a lot of side canyons there are, for if all were straightened out and placed end to end, there would be several thousand miles of canyon. And there are a lot of buttes, few if any of which are difficult of ascent for mammals other than man).

The variety of mammals in Grand Canyon is as great as the variety of habitats found therein: from beaver and otter in the deepest part of the canyon to red squirrels and tufted-eared squirrels in the coniferous forests, from desert-dwelling kangaroo rats to forest-inhabiting meadow voles, from rarely seen shrews to often-seen deer. The ubiquitous rock squirrel is found almost throughout the canyon. Mammals are abundant at any given place, perhaps as many as forty per acre and far more numerous than birds. The casual observer would not suspect this, but since so many mammals are nocturnal, they are not seen unless special search is made for them at night.

Herein is the story of the mammals found within Grand Canyon National Park. The story is not definitive, for mammalian exploration has not been done in the more remote parts of the park. This remains a project for future naturalists. The objective here is to review our knowledge of the seventy-four species that are known to be present in the park as of this date. For most, their distribution is mapped: known records are indicated by a symbol on a map and the probable range by a shading. The localities where specimens have been collected and preserved are recorded in a later section. Information on the habits and habitats of each species is included as far as it is available and space permits.

HABITATS AND BIOTIC COMMUNITIES

Within the Grand Canyon there are several areas that have a uniqueness of kinds of plants and animals. These may be called biotic communities. The major ones in Grand Canyon are listed below. These communities are best defined and delimited by their plant species. A map (pp. 14-15) shows the distribution of each community. Many of the plants and animals that characterize a given community are not necessarily found exclusively there but reach their greatest abundance therein.

Many physical factors are involved in delimiting such communities: temperature, humidity, rainfall, snowfall, and substrate, to mention a few. Climatological data from weather stations within the Inner Gorge and on the South and North rims (see table) indicate some of the diversity in climate within the park. These, in part, contribute to the diversity in plant and animal communities. Extremes in elevation in short distances do also. Although all of the communities except the spruce-fir and mountain grassland are duplicated north and south of the Colorado River, there is much isolation caused by the river and Inner Gorge. There may be less isolation in the riparian community, which is found along the Colorado River, than in the others.

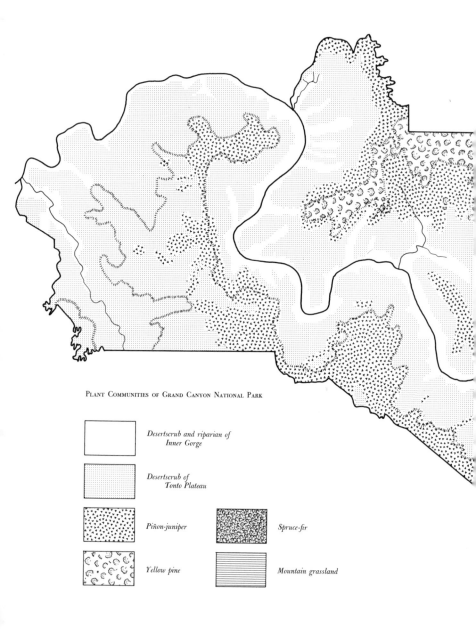

PLANT COMMUNITIES OF GRAND CANYON NATIONAL PARK

Desertscrub and riparian of
Inner Gorge

Desertscrub of
Tonto Plateau

Piñon-juniper

Spruce-fir

Yellow pine

Mountain grassland

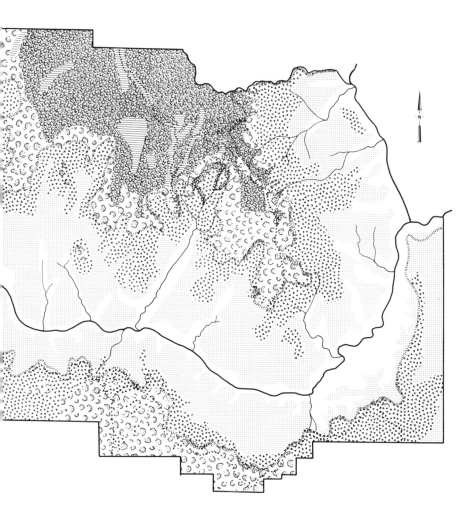

Weather station and elevation	Community	Average growing season (days)	Average annual precipitation (inches)	Average number days with 0.01 inches or more precipitation	Average annual snowfall (inches)	Average snowfall in Dec., Jan., Feb. (inches)	Average high temp. °F in July	Average low temp. °F in Jan.
Inner Gorge, 2,500 ft.	Desertscrub-riparian	275	13.01	58	6.3	6.3	109.3	25.0
South Rim Village, 6,930 ft.	Piñon–juniper–yellow pine ecotone	141	16.71	66	60.6	40.7	93.0	−1.1
Big Spring, North Rim, Kaibab Plateau, 6,600 ft.	Piñon-juniper	119	17.70	57	68.0	33.3	91.8	5.5
Bright Angel, North Rim, 8,400 ft.	Yellow pine–fir ecotone	96	28.04	78	140.1	108.8	86.5	−8.2

Desertscrub of Inner Gorge

The plant community of desertscrub within the Inner Gorge and canyons tributary to the Colorado River includes:

Catclaw	*Acacia greggii*
Mesquite	*Prosopis juliflora*
Saltbush	*Atriplex canescens*
Krameria	*Krameria parvifolia*

Riparian of Inner Gorge

The riparian community includes:

Cottonwood	*Populus fremontii*
Willow	*Salix lasiolepis*
Desertwillow	*Chilopsis linearis*
Tamarix	*Tamarix pentandra*

Some mammals of the desertscrub and riparian community in Grand Canyon are:

Spotted skunk	*Spilogale putorius*
Ringtail	*Bassariscus astutus*
Rock pocket mouse	*Perognathus intermedius*
Long-tailed pocket mouse	*Perognathus formosus*
River otter	*Lutra canadensis*
Raccoon	*Procyon lotor*
Beaver	*Castor canadensis*
Yuma myotis	*Myotis yumanensis*

DESERTSCRUB COMMUNITY OF THE TONTO PLATEAU

Above the Inner Gorge there is a bench or platform usually called the Tonto Plateau. This area contains the flattest continuum within the canyon, in places a mile wide, and it extends along both sides of the river above the Inner Gorge throughout the park. The plateau is mostly below 4,500 feet and is interrupted by numerous canyons. The predominant plant of this community is blackbrush.

Blackbrush	*Coleogyne ramosissima*
Desert thorn	*Lycium pallidum*
Bursage	*Franseria eriocentra*
Agave or mescal	*Agave utahensis*
Narrowleaf yucca	*Yucca angustissima*

Some mammals of the desertscrub of the Tonto Plateau are:

White-tailed antelope squirrel	*Ammospermophilus leucurus*
Cliff chipmunk	*Eutamias dorsalis*
Canyon mouse	*Peromyscus crinitus*
Cactus mouse	*Peromyscus eremicus*
Desert wood rat	*Neotoma lepida*
White-throated wood rat	*Neotoma albigula*
Bighorn	*Ovis canadensis*
Desert shrew	*Notiosorex crawfordi*
Ord's kankaroo rat	*Dipodomys ordii*
Silky pocket mouse	*Perognathus flavus*
Ringtail	*Bassariscus astutus*

Desertscrub of Tonto Plateau

Spotted skunk	*Spilogale putorius*
Rock squirrel	*Spermophilus variegatus*
Spotted ground squirrel	*Spermophilus spilosoma*
Gunnison's prairie dog	*Cynomys gunnisoni*
Black-tailed jack rabbit	*Lepus californicus*
Short-tailed grasshopper mouse	*Onychomys leucogaster*

Piñon-juniper woodland

PIÑON-JUNIPER COMMUNITY

A woodland that consists primarily of piñon and juniper occurs along each rim above the canyon walls and on some of the buttes within the canyon. The piñon-juniper community forms a belt between the yellow pine woodland and the desertscrub. The piñon-juniper community requires less water (the rainfall is usually 10 to 20 inches annually) and warmer weather than yellow pine woodland. Some plants of this community are:

Piñon	*Pinus edulis*
Utah juniper	*Juniperus osteosperma*
Cliff rose	*Cowania mexicana*
Broadleaf yucca	*Yucca baccata*
Serviceberry	*Amelanchier utahensis*
Rabbitbrush	*Chrysothamnus nauseosus*
Blue grama	*Bouteloua gracilis*
Ephedra	*Ephedra viridis*

Some mammals found in the piñon-juniper association are:

Piñon mouse	*Peromyscus truei*
Desert cottontail	*Sylvilagus audubonii*
Stephen's wood rat	*Neotoma stephensi*
Mountain lion	*Felis concolor*
Rock squirrel	*Spermophilus variegatus*
Cliff chipmunk	*Eutamias dorsalis*
Gray fox	*Urocyon cinereoargenteus*
Mule deer	*Odocoileus hemionus* (winter)

YELLOW PINE COMMUNITY

The yellow or ponderosa pine community is extensive on the North Rim, less so on the South Rim. On the North Rim this community is mostly between 7,200 and 8,200 feet, on the South Rim between 7,000 and 7,400 feet. Since this forest is open, grasses usually are present. Rainfall is usually more than 20 inches annually and the mean temperature during the growing season is about 60° F. Yellow pines occur as an isolated stand on Shiva Temple and nearly isolated on Powell Plateau. Although the yellow pine forest is small on the South Rim, extensive forests are found contiguous to the south of the park boundary.

Some plants of this community are:

Yellow (ponderosa) pine	*Pinus ponderosa*
Locust	*Robinia neomexicana*

Yellow pine woodland

Gambel oak	*Quercus gambelii*
Mountain mahogany	*Cercocarpus montanus*
Blue elderberry	*Sambucus glauca*
Creeping mahonia	*Berberis repens*
Fescue	*Festuca arizonica, F. ovina*

Some mammals of the yellow pine forest are:

Abert squirrel	*Sciurus aberti*
Kaibab squirrel	*Sciurus kaibabensis*
Merriam's shrew	*Sorex merriami*
Striped skunk	*Mephitis mephitis*
Uinta chipmunk	*Eutamias umbrinus*
Golden-mantled ground squirrel	*Spermophilus lateralis*
Mexican wood rat	*Neotoma mexicana*
Bushy-tailed wood rat	*Neotoma cinerea*
Mexican vole	*Microtus mexicanus*
Porcupine	*Erethizon dorsatum*
Nuttall's cottontail	*Sylvilagus nuttallii*
Mountain lion	*Felis concolor*
Deer mouse	*Peromyscus maniculatus*
Mule deer	*Odocoileus hemionus* (summer)

SPRUCE-FIR COMMUNITY

A spruce-fir forest with an intermixing of aspens occurs on the North Rim and continues northward onto the Kaibab Plateau. It is an area of heavy snowfall, cold winters, and a growing season of about three months. This area is isolated from other spruce-fir forests. The canopy of the forest is not open and in many places there is little growth of herbs and grasses but an increased growth of mosses and lichens. Spruces and firs occur mostly above 8,200 feet.

Some plants of this community are:

Engelmann spruce	*Picea engelmannii*
Blue spruce	*Picea pungens*
Douglas fir	*Pseudotsuga menziesii glauca*
White fir	*Abies concolor*
Aspen	*Populus tremuloides*
Mountain ash	*Sorbus dumosa*

Some mammals found in the spruce-fir forest are:

Red squirrel	*Tamiasciurus hudsonicus*
Northern pocket gopher	*Thomomys talpoides*

Spruce-fir woodland

Dwarf shrew	*Sorex nanus*
Long-eared myotis	*Myotis evotis*
Long-tailed vole	*Microtus longicaudus*
Porcupine	*Erethizon dorsatum*
Uinta chipmunk	*Eutamias umbrinus*

Meadows or mountain grasslands are present in limited numbers on the North Rim. They appear as open, shallow valleys, free of trees, with a large variety of grasses and forbs that are surrounded by spruce, fir, and aspen. Soil moisture is high as a result of the melting of a heavy snow cover.

Some of the plants in these grasslands are:

Mountain muhly	*Muhlenbergia montana*
Blue grama	*Bouteloua gracilis*
Black dropseed	*Sporobolus interruptus*
Squirreltail	*Sitanion hystrix*
Pine dropseed	*Blepharoneuron tricholepis*

Some mammals are:

Long-tailed vole	*Microtus longicaudus*
Northern pocket gopher	*Thomomys talpoides*
Long-tailed weasel	*Mustela frenata*
Least chipmunk	*Eutamias minimus*
Uinta chipmunk	*Eutamias umbrinus*

Mountain grassland

MAMMALIAN DISTRIBUTION
WITHIN THE PARK

Some species of mammals in Grand Canyon are found only on the north side, that is, north of the Colorado River on the North Rim, while some other species are found only on the south side. Some have speculated that the Colorado River or the canyon within the park, or both, has served as an effective barrier in mammalian dispersal. The absence of species on one side of the canyon may be because suitable habitat is not available. Only the North Rim has a spruce-fir and a mountain grassland community and the mammals associated with them. Still other factors may be involved.

First, one must establish how long the gorge has been the barrier that it is today. The canyon has been in the process of formation for about the last ten and a half million years. However, the main cutting of the canyon has been since the beginning of the Pleistocene or Ice Age, or slightly before. This may have been about three million years before present time. The cutting was done by the Colorado River while there was a gradual but continual uplifting of the terrain. By the middle of the Pleistocene the canyon was about 4,000 feet deep or, to put it another way, there had been about 4,000 feet of uplift with effective cutting by the Colorado River. By about a million years ago the canyon was cut to about its present depth.

All of this does not mean that the canyon has been the same barrier for the last one or two million years that it is today. During the Pleistocene there were extreme fluctuations in climatic conditions. There were long periods of extremely cold weather with extensive glaciers to the north of Grand Canyon, increased precipitation with subsequent heavy runoff and flooding, and eventually warm, dry conditions. This sequence of events was repeated several times. During periods of glaciation the canyon was much cooler than today and it is likely that as late as the Wisconsin glaciation, some 75,000 years ago, coniferous forests occurred throughout the canyon. The last glacial advance of the Wisconsin period was as recently as 20,000 years ago, and conditions even then must have been more boreal than at the present time. From time to time during the Pleistocene conditions were such that mammals of any given plant community could have shifted down the canyon to the river's edge, and if they could get across, conditions on the other side would be comparable and compatible.

At some times during the Pleistocene the Colorado River was a far greater barrier than it is today, for it must have been many times wider, perhaps miles wide, during periods of extreme melting, runoff, and rain. Even though some species were able to move down the canyon, they now found the river to be a formidable barrier. Perhaps if forests grew along the river's edge, there would be an increased likelihood that some trees, when washed out, might raft animals from one side to the other.

To review, during the last two million years, and perhaps longer, the canyon and the river may have been a barrier to the dispersal of some mammals, and the physical impediments caused by this ever-deepening gorge were complicated by the climatic changes of the Pleistocene — increased cold and boreal conditions, increased precipitation, exceedingly heavy flooding and runoff, and prolonged periods of warm, dry conditions.

In spite of all this, only eleven species are found solely on the north side, at least four of these because comparable habitat is not present on the south side. Fourteen species are found only on the south side. Of these twenty-five species (eleven to the north, fourteen to the south), thirteen have successfully crossed the Colorado River at other places, for elsewhere than in Grand Canyon they are known to occur on both sides of the river.

Perhaps the most striking example, if not the only example, of differentiation occurring within the park resulting in species-distinction is that of the Kaibab squirrel and the Abert squirrel. To many scientists the amount of differentiation between these two is not great — primarily a few color differences — but this may be in keeping with the incomplete barrier between the two sides of the river.

Species North of River

Dwarf shrew	*Sorex nanus**
Nuttall's cottontail	*Sylvilagus nuttallii*
Golden-mantled ground squirrel	*Spermophilus [Callospermophilus] lateralis*
Least chipmunk	*Eutamias minimus**
Uinta chipmunk	*Eutamias umbrinus**
Kaibab squirrel	*Sciurus kaibabensis*
Red squirrel	*Tamiasciurus hudsonicus**
Northern pocket gopher	*Thomomys talpoides*
Long-tailed pocket mouse	*Perognathus formosus*
Bushy-tailed wood rat	*Neotoma cinerea*
Long-tailed vole	*Microtus longicaudus*

Species South of River

Desert shrew	*Notiosorex crawfordi*†
Desert cottontail	*Sylvilagus audubonii*†
Spotted ground squirrel	*Spermophilus [Citellus] spilosoma**
Gunnison's prairie dog	*Cynomys gunnisoni**
Abert squirrel	*Sciurus aberti*
Common pocket gopher	*Thomomys bottae*†
Silky pocket mouse	*Perognathus flavus**
Rock pocket mouse	*Perognathus intermedius*
Ord's kangaroo rat	*Dipodomys ordii*†
Short-tailed grasshopper mouse	*Onychomys leucogaster*†
Stephen's wood rat	*Neotoma stephensi*
White-throated wood rat	*Neotoma albigula*
Mexican wood rat	*Neotoma mexicana*
Mexican vole	*Microtus mexicanus*

Some species of mammals that are found on both sides of the river have differentiated, by current interpretation, into distinct subspecies on the north and on the south.

* Present on north side (or on south side) because comparable habitat not available.
† Primarily, but not exclusively, south of the river.

Species	Subspecies north of river	Subspecies south of river
Bassariscus astutus	*nevadensis*[1]	*arizonensis*[1]
Mustela frenata	*nevadensis*[1]	*arizonensis*[1]
Spilogale putorius	*gracilis*	*leucoparia*
Canis lupus	*youngi*	*mogollonensis*
Felis concolor	*kaibabensis*	*azteca*
Spermophilus [*Citellus*] *variegatus*	*utah*[1]	*grammurus*[1]
Eutamias dorsalis	*utahensis*	*dorsalis*
Thomomys bottae	*boreorarius*	*fulvus*
Dipodomys ordii	*cupidineus*[2]	*chapmani*
Onychomys leucogaster	*melanophrys*[2]	*fuliginosus*
Neotoma lepida	*monstrabilis*	*devia*
Erethizon dorsatum	*epixanthum*	*couesi*

Twenty-two species of mammals occur within less than 100 miles of Grand Canyon, but they do not reach the park. For ten of these, suitable habitat seemingly is present within the park; for the other twelve, suitable habitat may not be present. Another twenty-seven species occur within about 200 miles of the park but do not reach it.

Certain species of mammals are restricted to the canyon and Inner Gorge of the park. These are less well known or less often encountered.

RESTRICTED TO BOTTOM OF INNER GORGE AND TRIBUTARIES

Raccoon	*Procyon lotor*
River otter	*Lutra canadensis*
Beaver	*Castor canadensis*

RESTRICTED TO INNER GORGE AND CANYON PROPER

California myotis	*Myotis californicus**
Ringtail	*Bassariscus astutus**
Spotted skunk	*Spilogale putorius*
White-tailed antelope squirrel	*Ammospermophilus* [*Citellus*] *leucurus**

[1] Subspecific differentiation not completely demonstrated.
[2] Different subspecies occurs *north* of the North Rim.
* Primarily, but not exclusively, here.

Rock pocket mouse	*Perognathus intermedius*
Long-tailed pocket mouse	*Perognathus formosus*
Canyon mouse	*Peromyscus crinitus**
Cactus mouse	*Peromyscus eremicus*
Desert wood rat	*Neotoma lepida*
Bighorn	*Ovis canadensis*
Burro	*Equus asinus*

* Primarily, but not exclusively, here.

CHECKLIST OF MAMMALS OF GRAND CANYON NATIONAL PARK

ORDER INSECTIVORA

FAMILY SORICIDAE

Merriam's shrew	*Sorex merriami**
Dwarf shrew	*Sorex nanus*
Desert shrew	*Notiosorex crawfordi*

ORDER CHIROPTERA

FAMILY VESPERTILIONIDAE

Yuma myotis	*Myotis yumanensis*
Arizona myotis	*Myotis [lucifugus] occultus*
Long-eared myotis	*Myotis evotis*
Fringed myotis	*Myotis thysanodes*
Long-legged myotis	*Myotis volans*
California myotis	*Myotis californicus*
Small-footed myotis	*Myotis leibii* [=*subulatus*]
Silver-haired bat	*Lasionycteris noctivagans*
Western pipistrelle	*Pipistrellus hesperus*
Big brown bat	*Eptesicus fuscus*
Red bat	*Lasiurus borealis*
Hoary bat	*Lasiurus cinereus*
Big-eared bat	*Plecotus townsendii*
Pallid bat	*Antrozous pallidus*

FAMILY MOLOSSIDAE

Free-tailed bat	*Tadarida brasiliensis*

* For subspecific identifications, see pp. 164-177.

ORDER CARNIVORA

FAMILY URSIDAE

Black bear	*Ursus [Euarctos] americanus*
Grizzly bear	*Ursus horribilis*

FAMILY PROCYONIDAE

Raccoon	*Procyon lotor*
Ringtail	*Bassariscus astutus*

FAMILY MUSTELIDAE

Long-tailed weasel	*Mustela frenata*
River otter	*Lutra canadensis*
Spotted skunk	*Spilogale putorius* [=*gracilis*]
Striped skunk	*Mephitis mephitis*
American badger	*Taxidea taxus*

FAMILY CANIDAE

Coyote	*Canis latrans*
Wolf	*Canis lupus*
Gray fox	*Urocyon cinereoargenteus*

FAMILY FELIDAE

Mountain lion	*Felis concolor*
Jaguar	*Felis onca*
Bobcat	*Lynx rufus*

ORDER LAGOMORPHA

FAMILY LEPORIDAE

Desert cottontail	*Sylvilagus audubonii*
Nuttall's cottontail	*Sylvilagus nuttallii*
Black-tailed jack rabbit	*Lepus californicus*

ORDER RODENTIA

FAMILY SCIURIDAE

Rock squirrel	*Spermophilus [Citellus] variegatus*
Spotted ground squirrel	*Spermophilus [Citellus] spilosoma*
White-tailed antelope squirrel	*Ammospermophilus [Citellus] leucurus*
Golden-mantled ground squirrel	*Spermophilus [Callospermophilus] lateralis*
Gunnison's prairie dog	*Cynomys gunnisoni*
Cliff chipmunk	*Eutamias dorsalis*
Least chipmunk	*Eutamias minimus*
Uinta chipmunk	*Eutamias umbrinus*
Abert squirrel	*Sciurus aberti*
Kaibab squirrel	*Sciurus kaibabensis*
Red squirrel	*Tamiasciurus hudsonicus*

FAMILY GEOMYIDAE

Common pocket gopher	*Thomomys bottae*
Northern pocket gopher	*Thomomys talpoides*

FAMILY HETEROMYIDAE

Silky pocket mouse	*Perognathus flavus*
Rock pocket mouse	*Perognathus intermedius*
Long-tailed pocket mouse	*Perognathus formosus*
Ord's kangaroo rat	*Dipodomys ordii*

FAMILY CASTORIDAE

Beaver	*Castor canadensis*

FAMILY CRICETIDAE

Short-tailed grasshopper mouse	*Onychomys leucogaster*
Western harvest mouse	*Reithrodontomys megalotis*
Deer mouse	*Peromyscus maniculatus*
Brush mouse	*Peromyscus boylii*
Piñon mouse	*Peromyscus truei*

35

Canyon mouse	*Peromyscus crinitus*
Cactus mouse	*Peromyscus eremicus*
Desert wood rat	*Neotoma lepida*
Stephen's wood rat	*Neotoma stephensi*
White-throated wood rat	*Neotoma albigula*
Mexican wood rat	*Neotoma mexicana*
Bushy-tailed wood rat	*Neotoma cinerea*
Long-tailed vole	*Microtus longicaudus*
Mexican vole	*Microtus mexicanus*

FAMILY MURIDAE

House mouse	*Mus musculus*

FAMILY ERETHIZONTIDAE

Porcupine	*Erethizon dorsatum*

ORDER ARTIODACTYLA

FAMILY CERVIDAE

Mule deer	*Odocoileus hemionus*

FAMILY ANTILOCAPRIDAE

Pronghorn	*Antilocapra americana*

FAMILY BOVIDAE

Bighorn	*Ovis canadensis*

ORDER PERISSODACTYLA

FAMILY EQUIDAE

Burro	*Equus asinus*

MAMMALS THAT MAY BE PRESENT

ORDER CHIROPTERA

FAMILY VESPERTILIONIDAE

Spotted bat	*Euderma maculatum*
Mexican big-eared bat	*Plecotus phyllotis*

FAMILY MOLOSSIDAE

Big free-tailed bat	*Tadarida macrotis*

ORDER LAGOMORPHA

FAMILY LEPORIDAE

White-tailed jack rabbit	*Lepus townsendii*

ORDER RODENTIA

FAMILY MURIDAE

Norway rat	*Rattus norvegicus*

ORDER ARTIODACTYLA

FAMILY CERVIDAE

Elk	*Cervus canadensis*

ARTIFICIAL KEY TO THE
MAMMALS OF THE PARK

This key is intended as an aid in identifying the more difficult or questionable species of mammals within the park. Those mammals that are well known and do not need special identification are not included: bears, lions, bobcats, deer, pronghorn, and bighorn. Since some members of the weasel and raccoon families may be confused, as well as the coyote and gray fox, these are included. Most persons can readily identify beaver and porcupine, but for completeness these two are included in the key for rodents.

SHREWS

Small size, with long, pointed noses and small eyes.

1. a. Tail longer than half the length of the body; ears not conspicuous in the fur; color brownish; five unicuspid teeth on each side of upper jaw.............................2

   b. Tail shorter than half the length of the body; ears conspicuous in the fur; color grayish; three unicuspid teeth on each side of upper jaw......................Desert shrew

2. a. Hind foot more than 11 mm long; underparts (abdominal fur) nearly white; greatest length of skull more than 16.5 mm..............................Merriam's shrew

   b. Hind foot less than 11 mm long; underparts gray; greatest length of skull less than 16.5 mm..............Dwarf shrew

BATS

Hand modified into a wing for flying.

1. a. Tail enclosed in interfemoral membrane (connecting legs with the tail) or less than one-twentieth of tail projecting beyond membrane.......................................2

b. Nearly one-half the tail projecting beyond the interfemoral membrane................................Free-tailed bat

2. a. Ears small to large but never exceedingly large; ear less than 27 mm long..3
   b. Ears very large; ear more than 27 mm long................8

3. a. Anterior or basal half of dorsal surface of interfemoral membrane not furred or only lightly furred................4
   b. Anterior or basal half of dorsal surface of interfemoral membrane well furred..................................6

4. a. Forearm long, more than 45 mm in length......Big brown bat
   b. Forearm short, less than 45 mm in length and mostly less than 40 mm...5

5. a. Fur on back drab gray; tragus (projection within ear) short, blunt, and curved; tooth behind upper canine when viewed from the side more than half as large as canine....
      .... Western pipistrelle
   b. Fur on back light brown to chocolate brown; tragus long, pointed, and straight; tooth behind upper canine peglike
      .... *Myotis* species
   (For characters to distinguish species of *Myotis*, see illustrations on pp. 52-53.)

6. a. Color of fur black with many hairs tipped with white (silvered); four small upper incisors with middle pair bicuspid ....Silver-haired bat
   b. Color of fur reddish, orangish, or brown; two small upper incisors, none bicuspid.................................7

7. a. Ears conspicuously edged with black; color of back dark brown with hairs conspicuously tipped with white...Hoary bat
   b. Ears without conspicuous edging of black; color of back reddish or orangish..............................Red bat

8. a. Color of back grayish brown; lumps on each side of nose; color of underparts smoky gray; four upper incisors......
      ....Western big-eared bat
   b. Color of back pale yellow; no lumps on nose; color of underparts nearly white; two (large) upper incisors....
      .... Pallid bat

1. a. Tail with conspicuous rings; scent glands not well developed...2
   b. Tail not ringed; scent glands well developed (weasel family) 3

2. a. Color on back grayish mixed with black; cheeks black with black extending as mask through eyes; bony palate more than half the length of the skull....................Raccoon
   b. Color on back honey brown; cheeks white; bony palate less than half the length of the skull....................Ringtail

3. a. Tail greatly thickened at base; toes webbed so that feet are paddle-like..............................River otter
   b. Tail not thickened at base; toes not so webbed that feet are paddle-like...4

4. a. Color black but interrupted with prominent white markings; underparts blackish; auditory bullae not inflated (skunks) 5
   b. Color brown or grayish brown; underparts orangish yellow or light brown; auditory bullae inflated..................6

5. a. White markings on back consisting of broken white stripes .... Spotted skunk
   b. White markings on back continuous, forming two stripes which are joined for much of the distance.......Striped skunk

6. a. Color of back brown and without stripe; underparts orangish; bony palate less than half the length of the skull .... Long-tailed weasel
   b. Color of back silvery brown with prominent single white stripe extending over the head nearly to base of tail; underparts honey brown; bony palate more than half the length of the skull..............................American badger

GRAY FOX AND COYOTE

1. Black hairs form stripe down top of tail, plus a black tip; lower jaw in side view with three notches at rear; legs about 9 inches long.......................................Gray fox

2. No stripe of black hairs down top of tail, although a black tip; lower jaw in side view with two notches at rear; legs about 12 inches long...............................Coyote

RABBITS AND HARES

1. a. Hind foot less than 110 mm and ear less than 80 mm long; ear shorter than hind foot; interparietal evident as a distinct bone...2
   b. Hind foot and ear more than 110 mm long; ear usually equal to or longer than hind foot; interparietal not evident but fused with parietal...............................3
2. a. Inside of ears sparsely haired; ear more than 70 mm long; anterior projection of supraorbital process blunted or denticulate..............................Desert cottontail
   b. Inside of ears well haired; ear less than 70 mm long; anterior projection of supraorbital process pointed.........
   .... Nuttall's cottontail
3. a. Tail black on top...................Black-tailed jack rabbit
   b. Tail white on top and bottom [may not be present in park]
   ....[White-tailed jack rabbit]

RODENTS

For convenience, rodents are keyed as four major (but not necessarily related) groups: (1) large rodents (beaver and porcupine), (2) squirrels, chipmunks, and prairie dogs (squirrel family), (3) large rats (wood rats), and (4) other rodents.

BEAVER AND PORCUPINE

1. Modified for swimming with fur long and dense; feet webbed; tail flattened; ear valvular...........................Beaver
2. Many hairs modified into prominent spines; feet not webbed; ears only slightly evident..........................Porcupine

SQUIRRELS, CHIPMUNKS, AND PRAIRIE DOGS

1. a. No stripe of black hairs on side which separates the darker-

colored upper parts from the underparts; tail well haired but not especially bushy; zygomatic arches converge anteriorly rather than parallel............................2

   b. Dark hairs form stripe (although short) on each side; tail bushy; zygomatic arches parallel with little convergence anteriorly (tree squirrels) 9

2. a. Sides of head without dark stripe; infraorbital canal present (ground squirrels and prairie dogs) 3

   b. Sides of head with three brownish or blackish stripes, with one stripe running through the eye; no infraorbital canal, although infraorbital foramen is present (chipmunks) 7

3. a. Tail shorter than one-fifth the length of the body; upper toothrows strongly convergent posteriorly.............
   ....Gunnison's prairie dog

   b. Tail longer than one-third the length of the body; upper toothrows not strongly convergent posteriorly..............4

4. a. Single white stripe on each side of the back...............5

   b. No white stripes on the back...........................6

5. a. Underside of tail reddish; cheeks and shoulders reddish..
   ....Golden-mantled ground squirrel

   b. Underside of tail white; cheeks whitish................
   ....White-tailed antelope squirrel

6. a. Tail more than 150 mm (6 inches) long; color grayish to blackish.............................Rock squirrel

   b. Tail less than 100 mm (4 inches) long; color yellowish brown, often spotted or flecked with white............
   ....Spotted ground squirrel

7. a. Dorsal stripes indistinct with only one pronounced median dark stripe...............................Cliff chipmunk

   b. Dorsal stripes distinct with several black and white stripes...8

8. a. Outermost dark stripes border the lateral white stripes, resulting in five black stripes; three middle black stripes narrow; total length usually less than 200 mm........
   ....Least chipmunk

b. No outermost dark stripes border the lateral white stripes so that there are only three black stripes and these are broad; total length usually more than 200 mm........ .... Uinta chipmunk

9. a. Size small, total length less than 400 mm ($15\frac{1}{2}$ inches); top of back dark yellowish gray; third premolar usually absent................................. Red squirrel
   b. Size large, total length more than 400 mm ($15\frac{1}{2}$ inches); top of back reddish or blackish; third premolar peglike but present...10

10. a. Underparts white; tail dark above...........Abert squirrel
    b. Underparts black; tail white above..........Kaibab squirrel

LARGE RATS

Large rats, as here considered, are all wood rats. The tail is about as long as the body and covered with hair (longer in some species); the ears are large; the tail is dark above and light below. For characters to distinguish species of wood rats, see illustrations on p. 138.

OTHER RODENTS

1. a. Tail about one-half or less of length of head and body (never more than 60 per cent)..........................2
   b. Tail more than three-fourths of length of head and body (always more than 80 per cent).......................6

2. a. External fur-lined cheek pouches; front feet with elongated claws for digging...............................3
   b. No external cheek pouches; front feet without especially elongated claws...................................4

3. a. Fur on sides orangish or reddish; length of dark patch behind ear about equal to size of ear; sphenoidal fissure in orbital region of skull.............Common pocket gopher
   b. Fur on sides yellowish gray or gray; length of dark patch behind ear greater than size of ear; no sphenoidal fissure in orbital region of skull...........Northern pocket gopher

4. a. Underparts whitish; hind feet white................. ....Short-tailed grasshopper mouse

43

b. Underparts blackish but often with a frosting of white; tops of hind feet blackish...........................5

5. a. Tail long, more than 40 mm and more than 40 per cent of body length; number of mammae eight....Long-tailed vole

   b. Tail short, less than 35 mm and less than 33 per cent of body length; number of mammae four.........Mexican vole

6. a. External fur-lined cheek pouches; hind feet noticeably longer than front feet and modified for jumping...........7

   b. No external cheek pouches; hind feet not noticeably elongated 10

7. a. Tail greatly lengthened (more than 130 mm); hind feet long (more than 34 mm) and soles densely furred; auditory bullae greatly enlarged.............Ord's kangaroo rat

   b. Tail long but less than 115 mm; hind feet less than 28 mm long and soles naked; auditory bullae not greatly enlarged...8

8. a. Tail only slightly haired and less than 70 mm long; conspicuous light patch behind each ear......Silky pocket mouse

   b. Tail well haired and more than 70 mm long; no conspicuous light patch behind each ear.......................9

9. a. Hind feet less than 24 mm long; skull short (about 25.5 mm) and narrow across braincase (about 12.5 mm); rump with some projecting spinelike hairs..Rock pocket mouse

   b. Hind feet more than 24 mm long; skull long (about 28 mm) and broad across braincase (about 14.5 mm); rump without spinelike hairs......Long-tailed pocket mouse

10. a. Upper incisors grooved on anterior face.............
    ....Western harvest mouse

    b. Upper incisors not grooved...........................11

11. a. Upper incisors with a distinct terminal notch when viewed from the side; belly, feet, and underside of tail usually dirty gray.........................House mouse

    b. Upper incisors without a terminal notch when viewed from the side; belly, feet, and underside of tail white....
    .... *Peromyscus* species

(For characters to distinguish species of *Peromyscus*, see illustrations on p. 128.)

ACCOUNTS OF SPECIES

SHREWS (Insectivora, Family Soricidae)

Shrews include our smallest mammals: smaller than mice with long, pointed snouts, velvety fur, small eyes, tiny feet, and ears nearly hidden in the fur. Only a few shrews get as large as rats, and none in North America. Shrews feed principally on insects and worms, foraging on the surface of the ground or beneath the leaf litter.

MERRIAM'S SHREW
Sorex merriami

Description. A medium-sized shrew with ears not quite hidden by the fur. Color, brownish gray above with the underparts, including the underside of the tail, nearly white or at least much paler than the back; feet whitish. Overall (total) length, 3½ to 4¼ inches (89 to 107 mm); tail, 1⅜ to 1⅝ inches (34 to 42 mm); hind foot, about ½ inch (12 to 13 mm).

45

Distribution.

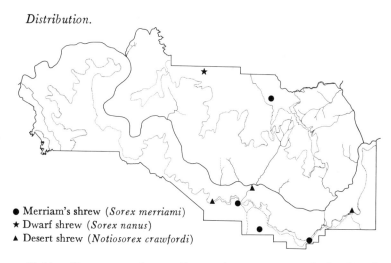

● Merriam's shrew (*Sorex merriami*)
★ Dwarf shrew (*Sorex nanus*)
▲ Desert shrew (*Notiosorex crawfordi*)

Habits. Shrews are the smallest and rarest mammals in Grand Canyon National Park. Merriam's shrew is one of three species within the park. It is found in coniferous forests, usually where it is moist and there is a good stand of grasses. These shrews frequent the runways used by meadow mice. They very well may feed on these meadow mice, for shrews are known to be ravenous feeders and in captivity will attack and kill mice much larger than themselves. Probably their chief source of food, however, is insects. Little is known of the habits of Merriam's shrews, and they are so uncommon that they have been taken in only a few places in Arizona outside of Grand Canyon. Judging from the habits of other shrews, we assume that Merriam's shrews are nocturnal, breed in late spring, have relatively few young each year, and build ball-like nests of rootlets and grass.

DWARF SHREW
Sorex nanus

Description. A small shrew with a fairly long tail, smaller than Merriam's shrew. Color, gray with a slight mixture of brown; underparts gray; underside of the tail definitely lighter than the top. Skull small with very small teeth. Overall length, about 4 inches (105 mm);

46

tail, about 1⅝ inches (42 mm) ; hind foot, about ⅜ inch (10 mm).

Distribution. North Rim. See map, p. 46.

Habits. The dwarf shrew is one of our rarest mammals. It has been found twice near the northern boundary of the park — once just inside the park (near Swamp Point) and once just outside at the Kaibab Lodge. In the Grand Canyon region the dwarf shrew lives among spruces and firs. Other than this, nothing is known of its habits. Elsewhere they are known to prefer rocky areas within the spruce-fir forests and feed on soft-bodied insects and spiders. The species occurs as far north as Montana, but usually they are rarely caught. However, at some places and at particular times they may be fairly abundant.

DESERT SHREW
Notiosorex crawfordi

Description. The desert shrew is grayish in color, short-tailed, and large-eared. It is the only shrew in Grand Canyon that will be found in dry places where there is sagebrush or cactus. Color, ashy gray above, slightly lighter below. Ears distinctly visible above the fur. Tail less than half the length of the body (in other shrews it is more than half). Overall length, 3⅛ to 3½ inches (80 to 90 mm) ; tail, about 1 inch (25 to 28 mm) ; hind foot, about ⅜ inch (10 to 11 mm).

Distribution. South Rim and south side of canyon. See map, p. 46.

Habits. Desert shrews are inhabitants of the arid parts of Grand Canyon. They prefer the areas mostly below the piñon-juniper zone and have been encountered in the sagebrush areas of Bright Angel Trail and Hermit Trail and the checking station at Desert View. Desert shrews are exceedingly rare and seldom seen. Two of the three specimens from Grand Canyon were discovered only by accident since they were found dead along trails.

Desert shrews feed on spiders, centipedes, and a variety of insects and possibly on other mammals. In captivity they require little or no water. They build round, birdlike nests beneath cacti, rocks, boards, or large plants. Young are born in late summer. Whereas Merriam's and dwarf shrews are inhabitants of the piney woods of the park, the desert shrew is the occupant of the hot, dry regions.

BATS (Chiroptera)

Bats are the only mammals that fly. Their arms, hands, and fingers have been modified into thin, flexible wings. The membrane of the wing attaches to the side of the leg and then continues to the tail. The wing and tail membranes are important in flight. The body of most bats is about the same size as that of many of our mice, although they are differently proportioned. Bats are barrel-chested with power-ful flight muscles attached to the chest. Eyes are small. Ears are of various sizes and shapes.

Within Grand Canyon National Park there are at least fifteen different species of bats. All feed principally on insects which they usually catch on the wing. Their erratic flight is the consequence of their pursuit of insects. While a bat is in flight, obstacles are avoided and insects are detected not principally by sight but by a type of sonar or reflected sound waves. The bat emits a high-pitched cry, usually inaudible to humans, and the time it takes the reflected sound or echo to be heard determines the direction and distance away an object may be. Each bat produces these supersonic sounds in its voice box, emits them through the mouth, and perceives them by the ears.

Bats are one of the few mammals that build no nests. Females of some species frequently congregate together when the young are born. In the Grand Canyon region myotis bats usually have but one young; the others have two young per year. Newborn and developing young cling to the mother with feet and teeth while she is at rest or in flight. If suitable caves or caverns can be found within the canyon, some bats may spend the winter there rather than migrating southward.

Since bats feed so extensively on insects, consuming much food each night, and since there are many thousands of bats in Grand Canyon during all but the coldest months, they greatly control insect pests. In the early evening, between sundown and dark, and again in the early dawn, numbers of bats can be seen flying on all but the coldest days in any part of Grand Canyon. They are the most conspicuous small mammals in the canyon.

YUMA MYOTIS
Myotis yumanensis

Description. This medium-sized bat is pale brown, being dull rather than glossy or bright in color, with pale-colored ears that are much the same color as the back rather than markedly darker. Feet large. Overall length, 3⅛ to 3½ inches (80 to 87 mm); tail, 1½ to 1⅝ inches (37 to 41 mm); hind foot, about ⅜ inch (8 to 10 mm); ear, about ⅝ inch (14 to 15 mm).

Distribution. Lower portions of the canyon, principally along and near the Colorado River and its tributaries. Common at Phantom

Ranch and in Havasu Canyon. Rarely reaches the rim of the canyon. *Habits.* Yuma myotis prefer the cliffs and rocky walls near water. From early evening until well after dark, they fly close to the surface of the water, both drinking and pursuing insects. When an insect is caught, the bat quickly takes refuge in the rocks adjacent to the water where it consumes the prey. Yuma myotis and California myotis are exceedingly numerous in the summer as they forage over the riffles in Bright Angel Creek between Phantom Ranch and the Colorado River. In Havasu Canyon they rest in the adjacent cliffs and, at early dusk, feed and drink along the creek. In the early light of morning and continuing until sunrise, they again can be seen hunting in the canyon. It must be infrequent that the Yuma myotis, normally an inhabitant of the desert regions of the lower canyon, reaches the wooded portions at the top of the canyon. However, they do get onto the South Rim and are sometimes found among the conifers.

ARIZONA MYOTIS
Myotis [lucifugus] occultus

Description. A large, dark, myotis bat with large feet, black ears, and broad snout or nose. The dark brown, almost blackish, hairs of the back are tipped with a brighter brown; the underparts are distinctly brown. Overall length, about 3½ inches (89 to 96 mm); tail, about 1½ inches (38 to 42 mm); hind foot, about ⅜ inch (8 to 10 mm); forearm, about 1½ inches (39 to 40 mm).

Distribution. Reported by Bailey as "South Rim."[1]

Habits. This must be the rarest of the myotis bats in Grand Canyon. Judging from its habits in some other parts of northern Arizona, one would suspect it to be found occasionally in the openings among ponderosa pines, firs, or spruces.

LONG-EARED MYOTIS
Myotis evotis

Description. A large myotis with especially long ears, large feet, and no fringe of hairs on the tail membrane (as in fringed myotis).

[1] Vernon Bailey, "Mammals of the Grand Canyon Region," *Grand Canyon Natural History Bulletin*, 1 (1935): 1-42.

Color of back brown, frequently with a golden cast. Overall length, 3¼ to 3⅝ inches (82 to 92 mm); tail, 1⅜ to 1¾ inches (36 to 46 mm); hind foot, about ⅜ inch (9 to 10 mm); ear, about ⅞ inch (20 to 23 mm).

Distribution. Common on the North Rim; Bailey's record from the "South Rim," locality not specified, might be an error.[2]

Habits. Long-eared myotis are common on the North Rim and seem to be closely associated with the fir and spruce forest. They move out of the forests in the evening to feed over the meadows and ponds. Usually the long-eared myotis is late in starting to fly, but on some occasions it has been seen well before dark. These bats are frequently found in the late evening hanging up in deserted buildings. They may have retired there to devour insects just caught. The especially long ears in these myotis must serve in part for the special reception of supersonic sounds.

FRINGED MYOTIS
Myotis thysanodes

Description. A large myotis with long ears, large feet, and a sparse fringe of hairs on the free edge of the tail membrane. Color of the back pale brown, of the underparts, silvery. Overall length, 3⅜ to 4 inches (85 to 101 mm); tail, 1½ to 1¾ inches (39 to 44 mm); hind foot, about ⅜ inch (8 to 11 mm); ear, about ¾ inch (16 to 19 mm).

Distribution. On both rims: rare on the North Rim, common on the South Rim. Not known from the bottom of the canyon.

Habits. Fringed myotis are late flyers among the bats and usually appear in openings among the trees and over ponds when twilight is turning into darkness. They are rarely seen in flight because of the darkness, but they sometimes may be encountered in abandoned buildings. Fringed myotis have one young in mid-June in the Grand Canyon region. During the daytime these bats probably find shelter by hanging in trees, in fissures in the canyon sides, and in attics or abandoned buildings.

[2] *Ibid.*

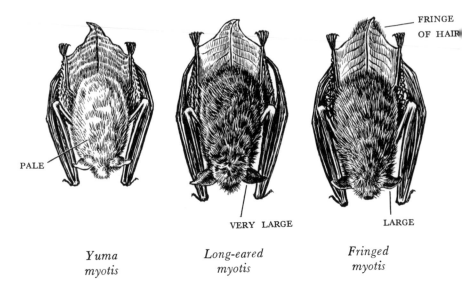

FRINGE OF HAIR

PALE

VERY LARGE

LARGE

Yuma myotis

Long-eared myotis

Fringed myotis

LONG-LEGGED MYOTIS
Myotis volans

Description. A medium-sized myotis with rich, dark brown fur, almost chocolate-colored, being almost blackish in some individuals. Ears blackish and not long. Feet large. A pronounced keel or fold of skin extending from the calcar, a process connected to the ankle and supporting the tail membrane. Color on underside chocolate brown with fur extending out on membrane as far as elbow and knee. Overall length, 3¾ to 4½ inches (94 to 107 mm); tail, 1¾ to 2 inches (43 to 49 mm); hind foot, about ⅜ inch (8 to 11 mm); ear, about ½ inch (11 to 15 mm).

Distribution. On both rims; more common among the pines of the South Rim. Not known from the bottom of the canyon.

Habits. The long-legged myotis and the western pipistrelle are the most common bats on the South Rim. Long-legged myotis are bats of the coniferous forests. Pipistrelles fly earliest in the evening but long-legged myotis emerge not too much later and can be seen flying over water tanks and openings in the pine forest before it is dark.

Only one young is produced each year and these are born in late June. Each mother carries the newborn bat with her as she feeds and drinks.

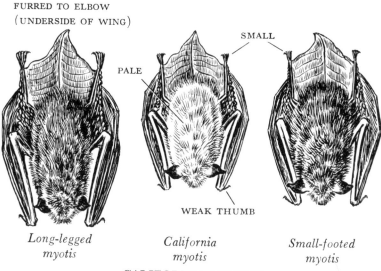

Long-legged myotis   *California myotis*   *Small-footed myotis*

CALIFORNIA MYOTIS
Myotis californicus

Description. A small myotis with a bright, light brown color, black ears contrasting sharply with the light brown color of the back, small feet, and a small thumb. Although the fur of the back is light brown, when it is parted, the fur appears black near the skin. Overall length, 3⅛ to 3½ inches (79 to 90 mm); tail, 1½ to 1⅝ inches (37 to 42 mm); hind foot, about ¼ inch (6 mm); ear, about ⅝ inch (15 mm).

Distribution. Bottom, sides, and both rims of the canyon.

Habits. This is the most common myotis of the canyon proper. It is abundant along the Colorado River and its tributary canyons and streams. It is not uncommon on either of the rims but is less abundant than the western pipistrelle and long-legged myotis. The California myotis probably inhabits by day the crevices in the canyon sides and normally feeds out in the more barren parts of the canyon. Some individuals, however, fly onto the rims to feed among the conifers. They start feeding rather early, both in the evening and morning. An individual captured and held captive for several days at Phantom Ranch ate during the evening twelve large moths, carefully cutting off and dropping their wings.

Young of California myotis must be born in early June in the Grand Canyon region. Juveniles, probably only a few weeks old, were found foraging for themselves in the second week of July.

SMALL-FOOTED MYOTIS
Myotis leibii [=subulatus]

Description. A small myotis, about the size of the California myotis, but color of back much darker, a chocolate brown, with a gloss or sheen; ears black but similar to the color of the back. Feet small. Overall length, 3⅜ to 3⅝ inches (85 to 92 mm); tail, about 1⅝ inches (40 to 43 mm); hind foot, about ¼ inch (7 to 8 mm); ear, about ⅝ inch (13 to 15 mm).

Distribution. Eastern portion of the South Rim.

Habits. The small-footed myotis is uncommon in the park. It has been found in the coniferous forest of the South Rim, frequently in association with long-legged and California myotis and western pipistrelles. Little is known of its habits in the park. On one occasion, it seemed to be an early flyer; on another occasion, it was found much later, flying about in a deserted building.

SILVER-HAIRED BAT
Lasionycteris noctivagans

Description. A rather large bat, blackish in color, with some of the hairs on the back and underparts tipped with silvery white; ears black. Feet large. Fur extends half-way out on the top of the tail membrane. In general appearance, this is a black bat with a frosting of white. Overall length, about 4 inches (98 to 106 mm); tail, about 1¾ inches (42 to 45 mm); hind foot, about ½ inch (9 to 12 mm); ear, about ⅝ inch (14 to 18 mm).

Distribution. Known only from Grand Canyon Village. May occur occasionally in the forested parts of the park.

Habits. Since only a single specimen, taken in September, is known from Grand Canyon, little can be said about its habits in the park. Elsewhere silver-haired bats frequent fir and pine forests, and one suspects they might be found on both the North and South rims occasionally, most likely in spring or fall when they are migrating.

WESTERN PIPISTRELLE
Pipistrellus hesperus

Description. A small bat (the smallest in Grand Canyon), pale
gray or yellowish gray in color, that flies early in the evening, frequently before the sun has set. The western pipistrelle is commonly
seen flying along the edge of the South Rim in the vicinity of the
Village and the points overlooking the canyon. The ears, wing membranes, and tail membrane are black, contrasting strikingly with the
gray of the back. Overall length, 2½ to 3 inches (65 to 77 mm);
tail, 1 to 1⅜ inches (26 to 33 mm); hind foot, about ¼ inch (5 to
7 mm); ear, about ⅜ inch (10 to 12 mm).

Distribution. See map, p. 56.

Habits. The western pipistrelle is the most common bat in Grand
Canyon. It is found throughout the bottom of the canyon and on
both rims. On almost any warm evening great numbers of pipistrelles
can be seen from the parapets overlooking the canyon. Along the rim-
walk adjacent to the El Tovar Hotel and Bright Angel Lodge, pipistrelles are the most conspicuous mammals, and they appear to be far
more numerous than the birds that are still present in the very late
afternoon and early dusk. In Havasu Canyon they are abundant along
the creek above Supai.

Western pipistrelles live usually in the cliffs and walls of the canyon. At most times they are more abundant within the canyon or

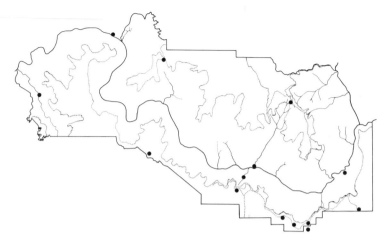

along its rocky rim than they are over the coniferous forests of the canyon top. Pipistrelles seem to be more numerous among the conifers when it is raining down in the canyon proper. On such occasions, they may seek other places to hunt insects and fly onto the dry rims.

At one time or another pipistrelles can be found flying over nearly every type of habitat in Grand Canyon: among the willows and cottonwoods of Bright Angel Creek (and around Phantom Ranch) and Indian Creek; at the water holes in Havasu Canyon; over the mesquite and creosote bush of the Tonto Plateau; over the sagebrush and piñon-juniper from Pasture Wash to Cedar Mountain; among the yellow pines of the South Rim; among the openings in the fir and spruce of the North Rim. In the summer pipistrelles may appear almost as early as 6 P.M., well before the sun has set, and some may still be flying in the morning nearly as late as 6 A.M.

Every year thousands of young pipistrelles are born and mature in Grand Canyon. The young, usually two in number, are born in late June or early July and are large enough to fly and feed by themselves in late July. A good proportion of the pipistrelles seen in midsummer are probably young of the year.

BIG BROWN BAT
Eptesicus fuscus

Description. A large, brownish bat, similar to the myotis but larger.
Feet large. Ears black; body fur varies in color from pale to chocolate
or rich deep brown, with the fur of the underparts slightly lighter
than the back. Overall length, 4¼ to 5 inches (107 to 124 mm);
tail, 1¾ to 2⅛ inches (44 to 53 mm); hind foot, about ½ inch
(9 to 12.5 mm); ear, about ⅝ inch (15 to 19 mm).

Distribution.

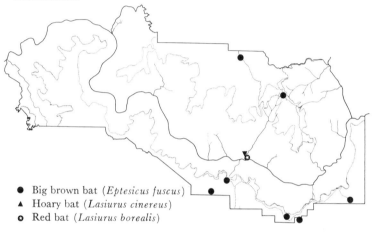

● Big brown bat (*Eptesicus fuscus*)
▲ Hoary bat (*Lasiurus cinereus*)
○ Red bat (*Lasiurus borealis*)

Habits. Big brown bats are the largest bats commonly found in the
coniferous forests of the North and South rims. In the summertime
they fly rather late in the evening over ponds and among the pines;
only rarely are they encountered in buildings. In colder weather they
frequent buildings more often. Big browns look like enlarged editions
of long-legged myotis and both occupy much the same territory.
Sometimes two big brown bats, possibly interested in the same insect,
will fight in mid-air. On one such occasion, park naturalist E. D.
McKee saw two bats crash in air and fall, somewhat stunned, one
into a muddy tank and the other onto a nearby rock.

Young are probably born in early June. Nursing females are found as late as the last week in June. It is possible that in winter big brown bats may move toward the bottom of the canyon to escape the cold.

Red bat

Hoary bat

Big brown bat in flight

RED BAT
Lasiurus borealis

Description. A medium-sized, reddish bat; the males are dark rusty red or brick red in color, the females yellowish with only a wash of red. In both sexes the wing membranes are black, the ears are short and round, the top of the tail membrane has a thin covering of fur, and some of the hairs of the back are lightly tipped with white (frosted). Overall length, $3\frac{7}{8}$ to $4\frac{3}{8}$ inches (98 to 109 mm); tail, $1\frac{3}{4}$ to $2\frac{1}{4}$ inches (45 to 54 mm); hind foot, about $\frac{3}{8}$ inch (7 to 10 mm); ear, about $\frac{1}{2}$ inch (11 to 13 mm).

Distribution. Known only from the bottom of the canyon (along Bright Angel Creek near Phantom Ranch). Probably occurs at times in other parts of the canyon. See map, p. 57.

Habits. The red bat is one of the most distinctively marked and rarest of the bats in the canyon. Its reddish color, narrow wings, and slow flight aid in recognition. Also, red bats frequently fly late in the morning, later than other bats. We observed one flying along Bright Angel Creek and among the cottonwoods as late as 9:30 A.M. and, on still another occasion, well after the sun was up. Some red bats spend the summer and probably breed in Grand Canyon. Whether they remain in the canyon in the winter, or migrate south as these bats do in some other places, is not known.

HOARY BAT
Lasiurus cinereus

Description. A large, dark bat with a frosting of white on the tips of the fur, giving a hoary appearance. The face, throat, and hairs on the underside of the wing are yellowish; the fur of the back and on the tail membrane, beneath the white tips, is mahogany brown. Ears are short, round, and rimmed with black. A distinctive yellowish-white spot is present at the base of the large thumb of the wing. Overall length, 4¾ to 5⅜ inches (120 to 135 mm); tail, 1¾ to 2⅜ inches (45 to 60 mm); hind foot, about ½ inch (10 to 13 mm); ear, about ¾ inch (17 to 18 mm).

Distribution. Known only from the bottom of the canyon (Phantom Ranch). Probably occurs at times in other parts of the canyon. See map, p. 57.

Habits. The hoary bat has been taken but once in Grand Canyon, and this in early April (5th) at Phantom Ranch. This might have been a migrating individual, flying northward for the summer, or a bat that wintered in the warmer parts of the bottom of the canyon. Much more needs to be learned about the hoary bat in Grand Canyon. On August 8, 1954, a member of our field party, Wayne H. Davis, saw a bat flying about the lights at the parking area of the Bright Angel Lodge on the North Rim. It flew at about 5 feet above the ground and circled the light standards several times. He was quite certain it was a hoary bat, but the individual was not collected.

BIG-EARED BAT
Plecotus townsendü

Description. A large, pale bat with large, thin ears and lumps on each side of the nose in front of the eye (thus the name, sometimes used, of lump-nosed bat). The color of the upper parts is tan; the underparts are considerably lighter. The ears are nearly transparent, and the inner or anterior margin of each is turned abruptly backward. Overall length, 3½ to 4¼ inches (90 to 107 mm); tail, 1⅞ to 2¼ inches (47 to 55 mm); hind foot, about ½ inch (9 to 12 mm); ear, about 1½ inches (34 to 38 mm).

Distribution. South Rim; probably on the North Rim also. Known for certain from only two localities. See map, p. 62.

Habits. Big-eared bats are late flyers and because of this habit are usually not seen. They commonly inhabit caves or mine shafts, but the few caverns of this type in Grand Canyon are seemingly without big-eared bats. During the night's hunt for insects big-eared bats frequently take refuge in deserted buildings to eat their captured food or to rest. At Grandview one or two of these bats might be seen flying leisurely in an abandoned building on almost any night in July after 10 p.m. At Pasture Wash the cicadalike notes of a bat, thought to be those of the big-eared bat, have been heard as they approached an old barn where big-ears take refuge in the loft. Here again, it was after 10 p.m. before the bats were seen or these distinctive "call notes" heard.

Big-eared bats probably give birth to young sometime in June. Females that were nursing young have been found from early until mid-July.

Mexican big-eared bats (*Plecotus phyllotis*) may be present within the park. They have been taken within 50 miles to the north and to the south. This species is sometimes called Allen's big-eared bat. It can be distinguished from the big-eared bat above by the presence of lappets projecting from the ears downward over the snout. It is a late-flying species.

Pallid bat

Big-eared bat   *Free-tailed bat*

PALLID BAT
Antrozous pallidus

Description. A large, pale bat with large ears and a simple muzzle (without lumps), large feet, and inner or anterior margin of each ear directed forward, not turned backward. The color of the upper parts is beige or yellowish drab, with some of the hairs tipped with dark brown (giving the fur a smudged appearance); the underparts are creamy white. The nostrils are surrounded by an indistinct horseshoe-shaped ridge. Overall length, 4 to 4¾ inches (101 to 122 mm); tail, 1⅝ to 2⅛ inches (40 to 53 mm); hind foot, about ½ inch (11 to 13 mm); ear, about 1¼ inches (32 to 36 mm).

Distribution. See map, p. 62.

Habits. The large-eared pallid bat is principally an inhabitant of desert regions. It is to be expected in the bottom and along the sides of the canyon. Likely places to see these bats are Indian Garden, Phantom Ranch, or Havasu Canyon. They can be seen in the late dusk flying among the cottonwoods and recognized by their large size and steady flight. However, pallid bats do frequently get out of the canyon and have been seen on both the North and South rims. On the rims they are always near the edge of the canyon, not far back in the coniferous forests.

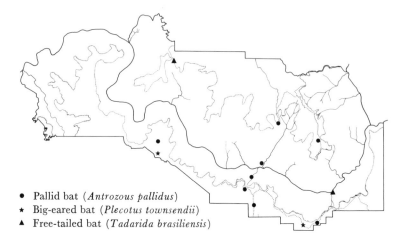

- Pallid bat (*Antrozous pallidus*)
★ Big-eared bat (*Plecotus townsendii*)
▲ Free-tailed bat (*Tadarida brasiliensis*)

Pallid bats are often found in sizable colonies in attics of buildings. They are not adverse to being crowded together in crannies and crevices. In hunting for food, they take insects both in flight and on the ground. One pallid bat, in an area just east of the canyon, was attracted by an insect on the treadle of a mouse trap and, when it swooped down to grasp it, was accidentally caught. Nothing is known about the breeding habits of these bats in Grand Canyon.

FREE-TAILED BAT
Tadarida brasiliensis

Description. A medium-sized, dark-colored bat in which the tail extends beyond the edge of the tail membrane (free-tailed), fur is short and fine, ears are about as broad as long, and the upper lip is wrinkled. The color of the upper parts is dark gray to smoky brown (almost brownish black in some); the underparts are only slightly lighter. Overall length, 3½ to 4¼ inches (90 to 110 mm); tail, 1⅜ to 1¾ inches (33 to 44 mm); hind foot, about ⅜ inch (8 to 12 mm); ear, about ¾ inch (18 to 22 mm).

Distribution. Probably in many parts of the bottom of the canyon and occasionally on the rims; specimens collected by us only on Muav Saddle, at the edge of the canyon, in the western part of North Rim.

Habits. Free-tailed bats are most rapid and high flyers. Bats with

62

long, narrow wings flying straight and rapidly or occasionally darting downward after insects in the hotter parts of the canyon may be free-tails. They often live in great colonies in caves (as in Rampart Cave along the Colorado River west of Grand Canyon), crevices in rocks, or attics of buildings. They invariably cluster together and great quantities of droppings accumulate wherever they roost. An unpleasant odor is produced by this excrement and by glandular secretions of the bats themselves.

Large numbers of free-tailed bats may live in unexplored caves or suitable crevices in the lower parts, probably of the western half, of the canyon. Free-tailed bats flying over Muav Saddle, on the western part of the North Rim, were apparently coming from much lower in the canyon. Free-tails are early evening flyers and frequently are to be seen with the much slower and smaller western pipistrelle.

Carnivores or Flesh-Eaters (Carnivora)

Carnivores are principally flesh-eaters that prey upon other animals and are adapted for hunting with their sharp claws and tearing or cutting teeth. Five families of carnivores are found in Grand Canyon: Ursidae, bears, now uncommon and transient; Procyonidae, raccoons and ringtails; Mustelidae, weasels, skunks, and otters; Canidae, dogs and foxes; Felidae, cats.

BEARS (Family Ursidae)

Bears are the largest land carnivores with short tails, large heads bearing small round ears, and a flat-footed walk. They are more nearly fruit-eaters than flesh-eaters. Members of the bear family are found primarily in the northern continents — only a few are in northern Africa and South America. The giant panda has recently been included in the family of bears.

BLACK BEAR
Ursus [Euarctos] americanus

Description. A large, black or dark brown, flat-footed animal, 2 to 3 feet high at the shoulders and with a short tail. All five toes of each foot are on the ground. Overall (total) length may be as much as 5 feet; tail, about 5 inches; claws on front feet, about 2 inches. Some individuals may weigh as much as 400 pounds.

Distribution. Occasionally in the wooded portions of the South Rim; possibly also on the North Rim.

Habits. The black bear is normally an inhabitant of the forested high country and more active at night than during the day. During the summer months bears usually spend the day bedded down in thickets. In the coldest parts of the winter they may become dormant and sleep continuously for several days, but they do not hibernate as ground squirrels do. They are omnivorous, eating as much or more plant material as animal matter, much sweet, ripe fruit, and they frequently tear open logs in search of adult and larval insects.

Black bears now are only infrequently found in the park. They most often enter the park along the southern boundary where a few bears are still present on the Coconino Plateau and within the southern Kaibab National Forest. In 1946 a small, brownish black bear moved into the South Rim area and was seen at Deer Tank in Cremation Canyon and its tracks found at waterholes in Long Jim Can-

64

yon. In May, 1947, tracks, perhaps of the same bear, were seen 1 mile south of Grand Canyon Village. A bear was reported crossing the highway in June, 1949, 4³⁄₁₀ miles east of Grandview and another in February, 1951, between Grandview and the Village. In June, 1931, a bear crossed the road at night near Pima Point in front of a car. Tracks verified the presence of the bear. Between June and August, 1959, a bear was seen at six places between the Village and Desert View. It may have been the same animal in all cases. In 1958 a bear was seen at the Village high school at 10 P.M. on October 7. Supai Indians formerly encountered and killed bears on the Coconino Plateau.[3]

Recent reports of black bears on the North Rim are lacking. When Vernon Bailey worked in Grand Canyon, he heard of a black bear killed about 1900 on the west side of the plateau at Swamp Lake and of another killed just outside the park about 8 miles northeast of the VT Ranch.

Black bear   *Grizzly bear*

GRIZZLY BEAR
Ursus horribilis

Description. Slightly larger than the black bear, with longer claws (3 to 4 inches) on the front feet and a pronounced hump above the

[3] L. Spier, "Havasupai Ethnography," *Anthropological Papers*, American Museum of Natural History, 29 (1928): 111-112.

shoulders. Brown fur silver-tipped (grizzled). Males may weigh as much as 500 pounds and have an overall length of 6½ feet.

Distribution. Presently unknown from park; possibly on North Rim in earlier times.

Habits. There is no proof that grizzly bears occurred in former times within Grand Canyon. However, grizzlies were present in the Pine Valley Mountains of southwestern Utah, and it seems possible that they ranged over the Kaibab Plateau to the North Rim. Vernon Bailey heard a story in 1930 of a bear, judged to be a grizzly, killed about 1860 or 1870 by a Paiute Indian in South Canyon on the east side of the Kaibab Plateau. There is an unverified report that Charles D. Walcott encountered a grizzly bear while studying Algonkian rocks in the eastern part (of the North Rim?) in the early 1880's.[4]

RACCOONS AND ALLIES (Family Procyonidae)

These are medium-sized carnivores which have ringed tails, walk with the entire sole of the foot on the ground (plantigrade), and are good climbers.

RACCOON
Procyon lotor

Description. In size and shape somewhat resembling a medium-sized dog, but distinguished by a mask of black over the eyes and a

[4] *Grand Canyon Nature Notes*, 8, no. 8 (1933): 214.

tail ringed with black and light bands of hair. The fur of the body is yellowish grizzled gray. The head is pointed at the nose, broad at the back, with rounded ears. The animals walk flat-footed. Overall length, 33½ to 37½ inches (850 to 950 mm); tail, 11½ to 16¼ inches (290 to 410 mm); hind foot, 5 to 5½ inches (124 to 140 mm).

Distribution.

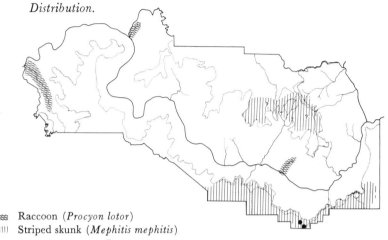

≋ Raccoon (*Procyon lotor*)
IIII Striped skunk (*Mephitis mephitis*)

Habits. Raccoons are highly dependent upon a continuous or constant supply of water and consequently are restricted to the lower parts of the park, along either the Colorado River or its larger tributaries. They are principally nocturnal and omnivorous.

The greatest numbers of racoons are to be found in Havasu Canyon. Their favorite food there undoubtedly is fishes, but they usually are unable to obtain these and turn to adult and larval insects or plant material. In Havasu Canyon raccoons must compete with the Indians' dogs for food, and the raccoons have been forced more and more to feed on wild grapes, berries, cactus fruit, corn, small birds, and bird eggs.[5] Raccoons den in the steep, rocky walls of Havasu Canyon and rarely if ever frequent the large trees that grow there. Some believe that this is a means of safety from their enemies and competitors, the semidomesticated dogs. It is said that Indians do not eat the raccoons but do use every means of keeping them away from their cultivated gardens.

[5] *Ibid.*, 5, no. 5 (1931): 49-50.

Raccoons are known to be present along Tapeats Creek and have been reported as far east in the park as Chuar and Clear creeks, but nothing is known of their habits there. There are no reports of raccoons along Bright Angel Creek but it is surprising that they are not present in this and similar creeks, especially where trees are present.

RINGTAIL
Bassariscus astutus

Description. Foxlike in appearance but house cat in size with a long, bushy tail ringed with black and white; legs short and body slender; eyes and ears large. Body color, grayish brown. Overall length, 24¾ to 29¾ inches (630 to 730 mm); tail, 11¾ to 15 inches (300 to 380 mm); hind foot, 2¼ to 2⅝ inches (55 to 66 mm). Weight, about 2 pounds.

Distribution. See map, p. 69.

Habits. Ringtails, or ringtailed cats as they are frequently called, dwell along the rocky walls of the canyon, where they skillfully climb over rocks and ascend cliffs. Occasionally they take up their abode in a building or a hollow tree. In the vicinity of Phantom Ranch ringtails are most abundant. Two young were captured in the dining room of Phantom Ranch and kept captive for a short time. Among the rocky cliffs they find many dry crevices in which to den and bring forth their two to four young each summer. When we were encamped

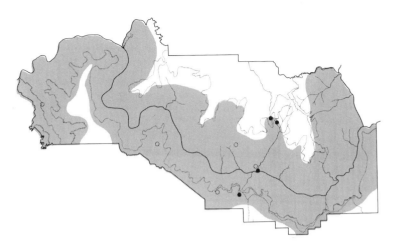

near the mouth of Bright Angel Creek, a ringtail unhesitatingly entered our tent during the night and made off with the mice and rats we had just caught. Ringtails also feed on fruits, insects, and birds and in general are quite omnivorous and opportunistic in their feeding. One I had in captivity also ate canned dog and cat food, bacon, hamburger, apples, and fish. It preferred raw to cooked meat.

That they may take up residence in buildings is illustrated by the presence of a family of ringtails living in the porch rafters of the house at Hermits Rest. For several years ringtails lived in the attic of the El Tovar Hotel and became so adjusted to this situation that they sometimes went into the dining room and took food offered by the waitresses. Our captive, taken adult, never became tamed. When cornered in the cage, it always bit our gloved hand but only did this at the beginning and thereafter submitted to stroking. Animals taken when young are reported to become more docile. Ringtails are seen from time to time around other buildings of the Village but are less often seen on top of the North Rim.

Tracks of ringtails have been seen at Bass Camp, in caves and around cliffs in Havasu Canyon, and along Chuar Creek. Since ringtails are nocturnal, they are not frequently seen but they must be one of the commonest, if not the most common, carnivores throughout the deeper parts of the canyon and gorge. In some places the spotted skunk may be just as abundant, but it is probably less widely distributed throughout the canyon. Ringtails apparently inhabit the isolated temples and buttes within the canyon, for their presence on Shiva Temple was detected.[6]

WEASELS AND ALLIES (Family Mustelidae)

Weasels, skunks, badgers, otters, and other members of this family are medium- to small-sized carnivores with poorly to well-developed scent glands, short legs, long tails, and sharp teeth. Most members of the family are valuable fur-bearers.

LONG-TAILED WEASEL
Mustela frenata

Description. A long, slender animal with short legs, long tail, and small, rounded ears. The summer pelage is brown everywhere except for a black tip on the tail, orange throat and underparts, and white lips and chin. The winter pelage is unknown in the park but one would surmise that some animals, especially on the North Rim, may be all white (except for a black tip on the tail). Overall length: males, 14 to 14¾ inches (355 to 375 mm), females, 11¾ to 13¼ inches (295 to 335 mm); tail: males, 5¼ to 6 inches (135 to 148 mm), females, 4 to 5 inches (100 to 125 mm); hind foot: males,

[6] *Natural History*, 40 (1937): 775.

1½ to 1¾ inches (39 to 44 mm), females, 1¼ to 1½ inches (33 to 38 mm). Males are larger than females, being nearly twice as heavy.

Distribution. On both rims; uncommon.

Habits. Long-tailed weasels are restricted to the wooded portions of the park and are not numerous on either the North or South rims. They are most likely to be seen on the North Rim. Although they are mostly nocturnal, they sometimes are abroad during the day. Little is known about the habits of the long-tailed weasel within the park. Elsewhere it is known to be a bold hunter of most kinds of rodents and rabbits. A specimen at The Basin, North Rim, was captured in the burrow of a pocket gopher, and one can surmise that here, as elsewhere, weasels prey heavily upon these burrowing rodents. A specimen taken at VT Park was attracted to a trap baited with a mantled ground squirrel. One litter of two to six young is produced in the summer. Possibly the weasels on the North Rim acquire the white ermine coat in winter. One specimen found dead on January 30 in the mule barns of Grand Canyon Village, South Rim, was brown.

RIVER OTTER
Lutra canadensis

Description. A stockily built, short-legged, thick-tailed, weasel-like animal that is adapted for living in water. The toes are webbed, the ears small, the fur dense but short, and the body streamlined for speed in the water. The long tail is thick at the base and tapers to a point. The fur is dark brown on the back and sides, slightly lighter on the underparts, and the head and neck have some gray intermingled. Overall length, about 50¾ inches (1,300 mm); tail, about 18½ inches (470 mm); hind foot, about 5¾ inches (145 mm). An adult weighs about 20 pounds.

Distribution. Infrequently encountered along Colorado River and its larger tributaries (Bright Angel, Havasu, and Tapeats creeks).

Habits. The river otter is exceedingly uncommon in Grand Canyon and very little is known about it. No specimen has ever been saved or photographed. There are less than a dozen reports of actual sightings within the park, but there are more reports of the presence of otter tracks. Since 1945 several otters have been seen: one swimming upstream in the Colorado River at the suspension bridge; one near the mouth of Bright Angel Creek; one in Bright Angel Creek; and one in the pool at the foot of Mooney Falls, Havasu Canyon. Kobe saw one about 1912 near Diamond Creek. Tracks have been seen along the Colorado River at such other places as the mouth of Tapeats Creek, near the mouth of Pipe Creek Canyon, above Parashont Canyon, and the lower end of the Hance Trail.

It is difficult to judge whether the river otter is a permanent resident in and along the Colorado River within the park or if it is a transient, carried down there by the powerful river. Otters are strong swimmers and under most circumstances must be able to sucessfully navigate the river. Fish in the Colorado and its larger tributaries must provide most of the food for these aquatic mammals. One expedition (Wing and Wohlmack) that traversed the Colorado River in 1951 reported cast-off catfish heads and droppings full of scales and fish bones all along the river. Mr. and Mrs. George McKinney observed an otter near the mouth of Bright Angel Creek frequently during the winter and spring of 1957-58, but it disappeared after a spring flood. The animal was playful and was seen to catch and eat catfish.

SPOTTED SKUNK
Spilogale putorius [= *gracilis*]

Description. A small, black and white mammal with a long, bushy tail, black except for the terminal fourth or third, which is white. The legs are short, head is weasel-like, ears are short. The four white stripes on the back and two on the sides are broken near the middle of the back into large "spots." A large white spot is present between the eyes. Overall length, 15¼ to 17⅛ inches (385 to 435 mm); tail, 5½ to 6½ inches (138 to 162 mm); hind foot, 1½ to 1⅞ inches (38 to 47 mm). Males (about 1½ pounds) are slightly larger than females (about 1 pound).

Distribution. See map, p. 74.

Habits. Spotted skunks are the commonest carnivores within the canyon, where they cavort in and around the rocks and cliffs and on the sandy beaches. The rock crevices, caves, and piles of fallen rocks make excellent hideaways and homes, but these small skunks never stray far from a supply of water. On almost any summer night spotted skunks can be heard and seen along Bright Angel Creek or Indian Creek and around the buildings at Phantom Ranch and Indian Garden. They are frequently noisy in their nocturnal wanderings and can be heard rustling through the underbrush or walking along the edge of a cliff.

In July and August, 1955, several spotted skunks each night passed

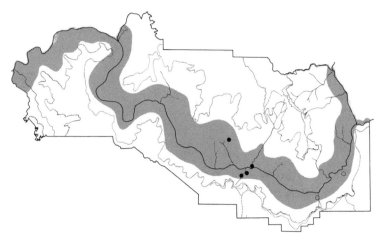

through the campground between Phantom Ranch and the Colorado River. They seemed to enjoy foraging under our cots. At the lower end of Tanner Trail, Glen Sturdevant and ranger Brooks found these skunks to be equally bold — one walked over them in their sleeping rolls and even pulled their hair. C. Hart Merriam, when encamped on the old Hance Trail, was disturbed by one sniffing at his head; he collected the specimen. The rock fences near Phantom Ranch and the trails adjacent to them are an especially good place to see spotted skunks. The trail-caretakers below Phantom have at various times made "pets" of skunks that lived near their rock house.

Spotted skunks are usually found only within the canyon proper — below 4,000 feet on the south, 4,400 feet on the north. There is a report, unverified by a specimen, of a spotted skunk seen crossing the road at Maricopa Point on top of the South Rim. Their presence on Shiva Temple was uncovered in an interesting fashion. One was found by Joseph Hall in 1963 in a large milk can that had been used by mammal-collectors twenty-six years earlier. Spotted skunks feed on beetles, grasshoppers, and other insects, mice, rats, and occasionally on small birds and eggs. That they sometimes use the burrows of rock squirrels is suggested by the presence at Indian Garden of four of these squirrels around a spotted skunk which was on the defense (or offense!) with its scent. Four to six young are usually produced in early summer.

STRIPED SKUNK
Mephitis mephitis

Description. A medium-sized, thick-bodied, bushy-tailed, black animal with a narrow white stripe starting on the nose, continuing over the forehead, and dividing into two white stripes on the middle of the back. Tail, with a mixture of black and white hairs, slightly shorter than the body; legs short but claws on front feet are long. Overall length, 23¾ to 26¾ inches (605 to 680 mm); tail, 10 to 12¾ inches (250 to 325 mm); hind foot, 2½ to 3 inches (64 to 73 mm). Individuals weigh between 2 and 4 pounds, with the males larger.

Distribution. Common on the South Rim; probably present on North Rim, but no records available. See map, p. 67.

Habits. Skunks on the rims of the canyon are the striped kind, larger than spotted skunks and with a distinctive odor of their own. Since they are so well protected with musk and powerful scent glands, they frequently are quite bold and take up their abode under dwellings and other buildings. At Desert View a skunk lived under an occupied house in 1953 and on more than one occasion wandered into the house when the back door was open. Earlier, in the summer of 1930, a female reared her five young under a house there. Three striped skunks lived at one time in July, 1954, under an abandoned shed at Grandview and could be seen foraging out from the shed in

75

the twilight of both night and morning. Striped skunks occasionally take up residence under houses in the Village. They do not hesitate to appropriate the dens of other mammals. These they may modify to suit their needs or use as found. Skunks can be good diggers. Striped skunks are not known to me from deep within the canyon and, although they are reported from the North Rim, there are no authentic records to date. There was a report of striped skunks in Havasu Canyon in the summer of 1970.

Young are probably born in May or June. Breeding occurs in February or March and the gestation is slightly more than two months. A female captured at Grandview on July 2 had given birth to young a few weeks earlier. Of the three skunks mentioned above as living under the shed at Grandview in late July, two were apparently the young of this female and the third, an adult male, may have been the father of the litter. Size of the litter may be as high as eleven with the mean around six. Several skunks lived under one of the buildings at the sewage disposal plant near the Village in 1927. Such a group, living together, usually represents a family unit.

Striped skunks eat a multitude of things including rodents, insects, carrion, eggs, berries, and nuts. Skunks sometimes gorge themselves on honey bees. An analysis of the food items in the stomachs of skunks in California indicated that the primary food items were insects, next grasses and roots, third rodents, and next birds. During the colder parts of the winter they den up and become dormant, but they do not truly hibernate. When winter approaches, striped skunks usually become fatter because food will be less readily available during the cold months.

Skunks are sometimes abroad during the daylight hours. Perhaps with the protection afforded by their scent glands they are less worried about enemies than are many other mammals.

AMERICAN BADGER
Taxidea taxus

Description. A short-legged, squat, broad animal with a short, bushy tail. General color of back silvery gray with a tinge of brown; white stripe beginning at nose, extending over head, and continuing along midline of back, sometimes to base of tail; face blackish with white cheeks; feet black; underparts yellowish and white. Overall length, 23¼ to 31½ inches (590 to 800 mm); tail, 4½ to 6¼ inches (115 to 160 mm); hind foot, 1¾ to 2¼ inches (42 to 55 mm). Adults weigh 15 to 20 pounds.

Distribution. Both rims, above the canyon proper.

Habits. The presence of badgers is frequently indicated by many large holes, about a foot in diameter, which they have dug in search of food — wood rats, ground squirrels, pocket gophers, prairie dogs, rabbits, and at times insects and snakes. These "diggings" are common in the piñon-juniper country from Desert View to Cedar Mountain and at many other places in the park. For example, they have been encountered at Yaki and Grandview points, on the road to Pasture Wash, at Grapevine Tank, and at the park headquarters building on the North Rim. When the prairie dog colony was present in Pasture Wash, badgers probably were present to feed on them and keep them in check. Judging from the number of badger holes, these animals must be common. However, one badger will travel extensively and make numerous "diggings."

Badgers are powerful animals, capable of digging at a rapid rate. The strong-smelling musk of their scent glands is rarely emitted by these animals. The remains of a badger found along the Colorado River at the mouth of Chuar Creek in December, 1929, might well have washed there from farther up the North Rim.

DOGS AND ALLIES (Family Canidae)

These are medium-sized doglike carnivores in which the tail is long and bushy, the hind feet have only four clawed digits, and none of the claws are retractile. The family includes foxes, coyotes, wolves, and dogs.

COYOTE
Canis latrans

Description. A long-legged, long-muzzled doglike animal with a bushy tail and long, pointed ears. The color of the back is a grizzled gray or buff with the sides a brighter color; the legs are a deep cinnamon color and the underparts a light buff. The ears are carried more erect and the tail lower than in dogs. The howl is a high-pitched "yip-yap." Overall length, 41½ to 49 inches (1,050 to 1,250 mm); tail, 7 to 8¼ inches (175 to 210 mm). Adults weigh from 20 to 30 pounds.

78

Distribution. Throughout the park; more abundant above the Inner Gorge.

Habits. The coyote is one of the most interesting carnivores to be encountered by visitors within the park. This close relative to our domestic dog is principally nocturnal but may frequently be seen during the early and late daylight hours. Their presence is made known at night by their weird bark and wailing howl, which may be coming from one or several coyotes. The coyote may be expected anywhere in the park but usually above the bottom of the canyon proper. Coyotes are nearly as abundant on the South Rim as on the North. They are to be encountered on remote buttes, such as Shiva Temple,[7] and to reach these places they must traverse some of the deeper parts of the canyon. But at Phantom Ranch the custodian in 1954, Slim Patrick, said that coyotes only rarely come that far down for water. Tracks of coyotes were seen at the mouth of Chuar Creek in September, 1931.

When hunting for larger game, coyotes usually work in pairs or threes. More than once when a single coyote has tried to jump a deer, the deer has driven the carnivore off by trampling it with its hooves. Within the park coyotes are known to hunt rabbits, squirrels, pocket gophers, and deer (mostly fawns) and to feed on juniper berries. In all likelihood, they feed on many kinds of mice, rats, birds, berries, insects, and even carrion. On the North Rim one coyote, called Old Rusty, scavenged animals killed by cars on the highway near Bright Angel Hill.[8] Coyotes are probably seen most often hunting deer, for then both the pursued and the pursuer cover great distances and frequently run near areas where people are present. More than once such a chase has taken both animals right through Grand Canyon Village. But for every deer the coyote preys upon hundreds and hundreds of small rodents and insects.

Coyotes bring forth their young in natural dens in rocky crevices or burrows in the ground. The average litter size is five. Young are born in April and May on the South Rim with pups being seen by

[7] *Ibid.*
[8] *Grand Canyon Nature Notes*, 7, no. 12 (1933): 128.

mid-July. It is not known whether the breeding season is later on the North Rim.

Some years coyotes seem to be more numerous within the park than others. This may be correlated with increases in small rodents which provide much of their food or with other favorable conditions. Just north of the park 305 coyotes were reportedly killed in 1908. Coyotes are still present in the national forest south of the park, and if their numbers are not too greatly reduced there, some will continue to drift on to the South Rim.

Coyote *Wolf* *Gray fox*

WOLF
Canis lupus

Description. Larger than a coyote, being about twice as heavy; ears short, head broad. Otherwise appearing much like a coyote.

Distribution. No longer within park so far as known.

Habits. In former years wolves were present on the Kaibab Plateau, although they were never abundant there. In the mid-1920's tracks thought to be of wolves were seen as far south as Jacob Lake and House Rock Valley. Some of these animals at that time or previously may have ranged onto the North Rim. As recently as March 3, 1948, assistant chief ranger A. L. Brown reported wolf tracks in fresh snow in the area of Bright Angel Point. There is the possibility that in the winter wolves from farther to the north may filter onto the North Rim.

Wolves formerly occurred on the Mogollon Plateau and probably in the San Francisco Mountains south of Grand Canyon. Since wolves have such long runways that they traverse while hunting, and if they were at all numerous in the San Francisco Mountains north of Flagstaff, one would expect them occasionally to have reached the South Rim.

GRAY FOX
Urocyon cinereoargenteus

Description. A medium-sized fox that appears dark gray above and reddish brown on the sides; a blackish stripe runs along the middle of the back and along the top of the tail to its tip; the backs of the ears are reddish and the underparts along the midventral line are white; the underside of the bushy tail is reddish brown. Overall length, 36½ to 41 inches (925 to 1,050 mm); tail, 15⅜ to 17⅜ inches (390 to 440 mm); hind foot, 5⅛ to 5⅞ inches (130 to 148 mm). Weight, 6 to 10 pounds.

Distribution. Throughout the park.

Habits. Gray foxes are to be found throughout much of the park, including the upper parts of the rims. Although their general color is gray, the reddish-brown fur of the lower sides has caused some people to call them red foxes, but no true red foxes are to be found anywhere in the park.

Gray foxes do most of their foraging by night, but frequently this extends over into the daylight hours. Gray foxes often are seen in mid-morning or late afternoon. They are probably seen more often than their sharp, rapid "yap, yap, yap" call is heard. Crevices in the rocky walls of the canyon, rock piles, hollow trees, and old badger holes provide den sites for these foxes. "Grays" are good climbers and frequently take to trees.

Gray foxes are known to eat a variety of things — mice, rats, squirrels, rabbits, insects, berries, and fruits. That they might possibly feed on spotted skunks is indicated by numerous fox tracks around the remains of one of these skunks near Red Rock Tank below Bass Camp. A "gray" with a mouse in its mouth jogged along the Kaibab Trail just below Yaki Point in front of a mule train.[9] This fox apparently denned near there, for a pair with half-grown pups was seen in June, 1927. Insects eaten include grasshoppers, crickets, beetles, and various grubs. Feathers in the stomachs of gray foxes indicate that they often feed on birds. They even feed on the fruits of the prickly pear cactus.

Red foxes (*Vulpes vulpes*) have been taken no closer than the area near Four Corners, nearly 200 miles east of the park.

[9] *Ibid.*, 2, no. 1 (1927): 2.

CATS (Family Felidae)

These are medium- to large-sized carnivores in which the face is short, the feet padded and with retractile claws, and the teeth highly specialized for cutting meat.

MOUNTAIN LION
Felis concolor

Description. A large, long-tailed cat in which the color in adults is *uniformly* tawny or light brown with the underparts slightly lighter and the tip of the tail and some markings on the face darker brown; the young are spotted with black. Overall length, 6 to 8 feet (1,830 to 2,440 mm); tail, 2 to 3 feet (610 to 915 mm); hind foot, 10 to 12 inches (255 to 305 mm). The weight of males may go as high as 275 pounds but usually is between 100 and 165 pounds; females are usually between 75 and 100 pounds.

Distribution. Throughout the park.

Habits. One of the most exciting mammals to be seen in Grand Canyon is the mountain lion, sometimes called the puma or cougar. This large cat will be encountered more frequently in the remotest parts of the park, but occasionally it is seen near the Village, along the roads, or at some of the observation points. A mountain lion was seen passing through the Village in 1919 and probably many have since then. However, these cats are more common along the southern boundary of the park than in the Village area. On September 15, 1958, one was seen chasing a deer near Hopi Point, and on July 6, 1963, one was perched in a large cottonwood just below Indian Garden. In 1954 we saw one at Hilltop on the western part of the South Rim. Mountain lions are far more numerous on the North Rim than on the South. This is particularly true for the western part of the park where large segments of the Kaibab Plateau invade it. In former years mountain lions were abundant on the North Kaibab where they served as a check on the mule deer. In 1909 one game warden took over eighty lions; in 1929 two hunters took ninety-six lions. In spite of continued killing of lions in this region, some still persist. Their numbers are so reduced, however, that they now have little effect in keeping the overpopulous mule deer in check.

In many places in Arizona mountain lions are inhabitants of the rimrock country. Here they lie in wait for passing deer. Since mule deer were never especially numerous within the canyon, mountain lions probably were never common there. However, those lions present could and undoubtedly did prey upon bighorn and upon deer that were forced into the canyon during the winter. A lion was seen to "jump" a deer along the trail one-half mile below Indian Garden several years ago. Most of the mountain lions in the park dwell in the forested areas — junipers, pines, and firs — and at present are commonest in the roughest, most unfrequented parts. Kittens, usually one to four, are born about March or April and cubs have been seen in the park in July and August. An adult lion will kill an average of two to three mule deer each week. Probably many kinds of mammals provide food when there is a need. Even the readily available but "sticky" porcupine may be killed and eaten.

Sometimes when a mountain lion is stalking game, it loses its regard for humans and can be approached rather closely. On one such occasion a caravan of sightseers, including several cars, was able to approach one lion on the North Rim within 150 feet as this cat was busily stalking a large deer.[10]

[10] *Ibid.*, 7, no. 5 (1932): 54.

JAGUAR
Felis onca

Description. A large cat, similar to the mountain lion but heavily spotted with black and heavier-bodied with thicker legs. General color, yellowish or orangish brown with "spots" consisting of rosettes of black patches; light underparts also spotted with black; tail with black bands or bars toward tip. The length is slightly less than that of the mountain lion but the weight is nearly a third again as great.

Distribution. Known only in former times (about 1907 or 1908) from "near the railroad about 4 miles south of the canyon rim."

Habits. A jaguar, often called tiger, the heaviest and most powerful of all our American cats, reportedly was killed at the above locality by a group of Indians. The late Major E. A. Goldman, prominent mammalogist, secured the information from the Kolb brothers in 1913. Major Goldman seemed satisfied that the animal was a jaguar. No specimen of jaguar has been preserved from closer to this locality than Cibecue, Arizona, some 170 miles to the southeast. It is reported that the jaguar in the park was an old animal with much-worn teeth but in fine pelage. It was tracked on the snow to where it had killed a colt.

The jaguar leaves a footprint with the toes more widely spread and less of the rear pad showing than the mountain lion. The jaguar usually does not cover its kill as the mountain lion will.

The jaguar is a more powerful animal than the mountain lion and is capable of killing much larger animals than the lion can. For example, jaguars are able to kill cattle, including adult bulls, and horses. Large jaguars may weigh nearly 300 pounds and measure nearly 11 feet long. Jaguars are rare anywhere in Arizona at the present time.

BOBCAT
Lynx rufus

Description. A medium-sized, short-tailed cat, slightly larger than a house cat, with pointed ears that have small, black tufts, and long legs. The general color of the animal is yellowish brown or yellowish gray, tending to be more yellowish on the sides, darker on the back, and whitish below; the underparts have conspicuous black spots, the sides inconspicuous reddish spots; dark, narrow, irregular stripes are present on the face, cheeks, and down the middle of the back; the backs of the ears are mostly black and the end of the tail is tipped with black. Overall length, 28¾ to 33 inches (730 to 840 mm); tail, 5 to 6 inches (125 to 155 mm); hind foot, 5 to 6½ inches (125 to 165 mm). Weight, 11 to 20 pounds; males are slightly larger than females.

Distribution. Throughout the park.

Habits. Bobcats, or wildcats or lynx cats as they are sometimes called, are so often seen in the daytime that a good many visitors in the park get a view of them. Since these cats are not readily frightened, being much bolder than mountain lions, they can frequently be approached quite closely by man and, conversely, sometimes closely approach man and his dwellings. They have been seen in the Village near the post office and at several of the observation points. One drank from the birdbath at Yaki Point. A bobcat was so intent on stalking a black-tailed jack rabbit on the road at Desert View that the cat sprang at the rabbit at the same time we drove by. The bobcat nearly hit the side of our car in its leap but at the last moment veered enough to avoid our car and also miss the rabbit. The cat made off into the junipers and out of sight, but the rabbit was so paralyzed with fright that it remained motionless — seemingly stupefied — in the road for many seconds after the cat had left and as we approached on foot.

Bobcats prefer broken country with cliffs and rock outcroppings as well as wooded areas, especially the piñon-juniper belt. The canyon is an ideal place for them. They hunt and den both within the canyon and on the two rims. Crevices and caves make ideal den sites. One cat on the North Rim had a den under the dense spreading branches of a blue spruce. Kittens have been seen in the park in August and probably were born in late spring. Within the park bobcats are known to feed on rock squirrels, mantled ground squirrels, cottontails, jack rabbits, wood rats, and tree squirrels. They probably also feed on ground-dwelling birds, pocket gophers, mice, and fawns. In former times they occasionally preyed upon young pronghorns. Bobcats are active the year around. They are capable of rendering weird and eerie yowls and meows, sounding somewhat like house cats but louder and huskier. These "screams" are most often heard during the mating season. Tracks of bobcats are frequently found at Indian Garden, Phantom Ranch, Pipe Springs, and along the trails within the canyon.

The true lynx, or Canada lynx, is not known to occur within the park. Vernon Bailey reported that a William Crosby of Kanab, Utah, told him his uncle trapped a Canada lynx 15 miles southeast of Jacob Lake about 1905. Whether this was a lynx or an especially large bobcat can not be ascertained, but there are no specimens preserved to indicate the presence of the lynx (*Lynx canadensis*) within the park.

RABBITS AND HARES (Lagomorpha, Family Leporidae)

Lagomorphs have a short but well-furred tail and long ears; locomotion is often by hopping or leaping, with the hind feet longer than the front. They have two pairs of upper incisors with the second pair peglike and directly behind the first. Young of rabbits (including cottontails) are helpless and hairless at birth; of hares (including jack rabbits), precocial, furred, and with the eyes open.

DESERT COTTONTAIL
Sylvilagus audubonii

Description. A medium-sized rabbit with relatively long ears (not nearly the size of those of the jack rabbit) which are not heavily haired, long hind legs, mottled grayish-brown color, and a short but conspicuous tail, white on underside. Overall (total) length, 14½ to 16 inches (365 to 400 mm); tail, 2 to 3 inches (50 to 75 mm); hind foot, 3½ to 4 inches (88 to 100 mm); ear, about 3 inches (75 mm).

Distribution. South Rim only. Possibly on North Rim around Powell Plateau. See map, p. 89.

Habits. On the South Rim there is but one cottontail — the desert or Audubon's cottontail. These cottontails are more often seen in early morning or late evening, often nibbling on the leaves of shrubs or grasses. However, they eat a great variety of plant materials. In turn, they are preyed upon by many carnivores including coyotes, gray foxes, bobcats, owls, hawks, and large snakes. A cottontail in the

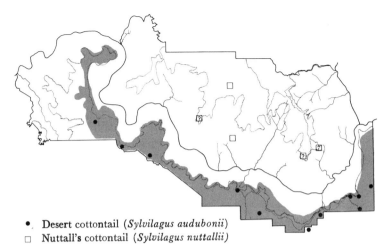

• Desert cottontail (*Sylvilagus audubonii*)
□ Nuttall's cottontail (*Sylvilagus nuttallii*)

grasp of a hawk that was barely airborne managed to escape and take refuge in the sagebrush about a mile east of the Village.[11] Cottontails have been an important food item for many years for the Indians of the park. In spite of all depredations, they are still common on the South Rim and are more abundant some years than others. Desert cottontails have two to six young per litter and probably more than one litter each year.

Two cottontails became associated with the small herd of semitame deer near the south village in the winter of 1929-30. This association was partly to take advantage of the barley and hay provided in the feed yard but also for the clearing and warmth provided, for the cottontails bedded alongside the deer and left the feed yard when the deer departed.[12]

At least one domestic rabbit (genus *Oryctolagus*) has been released within the park and was living in the wild in 1931, according to ranger Burt Lurzon.[13] This rabbit was associated with three deer (it actually was seen resting on the back of one bedded-down deer) in the piñon forest. Such introductions of nonnative mammals should be avoided.

[11] *Ibid.*, 2, no. 9 (1928): 7.
[12] *Ibid.*, 4, no. 5 (1930): 32.
[13] *Ibid.*, 5, no. 4 (1931): 38.

NUTTALL'S COTTONTAIL
Sylvilagus nuttallii

Description. A smallish rabbit with much the same appearance as the desert cottontail, except slightly smaller, ears smaller, and animals usually much shyer. Overall length, about 15 inches (380 mm); tail, 1½ to 2 inches (40 to 50 mm); hind foot, about 3¾ inches (95 mm); ears, about 2½ inches (65 mm).

Distribution. North Rim, especially in sagebrush flats, and Shiva Temple. See map, p. 89.

Habits. Nuttall's cottontails are infrequently seen inhabitants of the sagebrush flats and gullies of the North Rim. Specimens taken on Shiva Temple and Crystal Creek are of this species. Cottontails seen at Neal Spring, Cape Royal, and the saddle north of Shiva Temple probably were Nuttall's also. One wonders what the cottontails on the North Rim do when the snow becomes exceedingly deep. This may in part account for their summertime scarcity.

Nuttall's cottontails find refuge in the rock piles and brush thickets. They feed on herbaceous material and have been seen eating juniper berries. They may have as many as eight young.

These cottontails, like desert cottontails, are primarily crepuscular — active in the twilight of early morning and early evening. Nuttall's cottontails often live in areas of large rocks or crevices, and on the North Rim may be associated with the bushy-tailed wood rat.

Young cottontails are reared in a nest, for they are blind, nearly hairless, and quite helpless at birth. Often the nests are placed in old burrows, under brush piles, or under rocks. The young are weaned at about a month of age. Young cottontails, dispersing from the nest area, provide a source of food for many kinds of carnivores.

BLACK-TAILED JACK RABBIT
Lepus californicus

Description. A large rabbit (actually a hare) with large, naked ears and long hind feet. Tips of the ears black; top of the tail conspicuously black. Overall length, 20 to 23 inches (500 to 590 mm); tail, 2½ to 4 inches (65 to 100 mm); hind foot, 4½ to 5½ inches (115 to 140 mm); ear, about 5 inches (130 mm). Adults will weigh up to 6 pounds.

Distribution. North and South rims, but uncommon on North Rim. Usually found in open brush country.

Habits. Black-tailed jack rabbits prefer open or semiopen country. Consequently, they are more abundant and more widespread in the unforested parts of the South Rim. Here they are to be found in numbers from Great Thumb Mesa and Hilltop on the west to Cedar Mountain on the east. Although they are not numerous on the North Rim, they may be more so in the western part on or near Powell Plateau.

Since jack rabbits are large and are active in the early morning and evening, they often are seen by the traveler. Even in wintertime these "jacks" are active and may be seen on and in the snow. They do not assume the light-colored winter pelage as does the snowshoe hare or as the white-tailed jack rabbit may.

Black-tailed jacks may have as many as six young per litter but the number is usually two or three. More than one litter per year can be expected. Young are fully furred and active at birth. Food consists of the leaves of bushes, weeds, and grasses. "Jacks" have an especially acute sense of hearing and their large ears are always alert and searching for sounds of possible enemies. They are preyed upon by all the larger carnivorous mammals, birds, and some snakes. The stalking of an adult jack rabbit by a bobcat is detailed in the account of the bobcat. A healthy jack rabbit can outrun most of its enemies. Many individuals are heavily infested with internal and external parasites, and these may slow the animal.

White-tailed jack rabbit (*Lepus townsendii*) is about the size of the black-tailed jack but has conspicuous white on the top and bottom of the tail and attains a white winter coat. White-tailed jack rabbits are not known to occur closer than Kanab, Utah, but some reports by interested observers of large, exceedingly wary rabbits, with unusual coats, seen in the remote parts of the North Rim may have been this species. Elsewhere white-tailed jacks are known to inhabit the flat-topped ridges at high altitudes, are primarily nocturnal, and hide among the conifers during the day.

RODENTS (Rodentia)

Rodents, the so-called gnawing mammals, have one pair, and only one pair, of upper and lower incisor teeth which are persistently growing and always sharp. Immediately behind these incisors there are no teeth in the jaw but, instead, a gap or diastema. Rodents are generally small but make up in numbers of individuals for what they lack in size.

SQUIRRELS, CHIPMUNKS, AND PRAIRIE DOGS
(Family Sciuridae)

Members of the squirrel family in the park have long, bushy tails, are of medium size, are active during the daytime only, and live either in trees or holes in the ground or crevices in the rocks. Included are ground squirrels, prairie dogs, chipmunks, and tree squirrels. Marmots may have lived within the park many decades ago, but their presence is unknown now.

ROCK SQUIRREL
Spermophilus [Citellus] variegatus

Description. A large, often-conspicuous ground squirrel with an overall appearance of gray resulting from a variegated pattern of black and white fur; lower back often appears reddish, especially when fur is abraded; tail bushy and same color as back. Because of their large size, they are sometimes confused with grayish tree squirrels. Overall (total) length, 17½ to 20 inches (440 to 510 mm); tail, 7½ to 9½ inches (190 to 240 mm); hind foot, about 2¼ inches (60 mm).

Distribution. See map, p. 94.

Habits. The large, bushy-tailed squirrels eagerly eating nearly any kind of food offered at various viewpoints along the rim, such as at Hopi and Yavapai points and the El Tovar Hotel, are rock squirrels. They are active from sunup to sundown but enter into a winter sleep — hibernation — during the cold winter weeks. As the name implies, they prefer a habitat with ample rocks and they nest in crevices down in the rocks or in holes near rocks. One nest was uncovered 3 feet below ground level at the Village. They sometimes

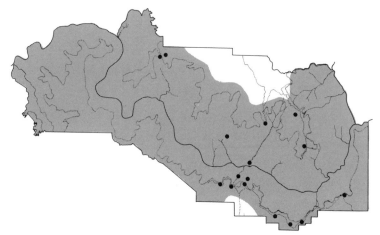

do climb trees and bushes, partly to survey for enemies and sometimes to seek food. On the North Rim rock squirrels in some places climb piñon trees, cut the cones, and shell out the nuts. One squirrel was known to store seventy-two piñon seeds in its cheek pouches. Some have been seen climbing Douglas firs to get at the cones and then descending the trees headfirst. At other places in the canyon rock squirrels feed on prickly pear cactus fruit, various seeds, buds, and leaves. But these squirrels really prefer rocky situations and consequently the rocky slopes of the canyon are no barrier to them. This is indicated by their presence on Shiva Temple and probably most of the other isolated buttes.

In Havasu Canyon rock squirrels prey heavily on the gardens and apricots that the Supais raise. The squirrels dig the succulent bulbs of the mariposa lily and eat on the asparaguslike stalk of the agave or century plant. Corrals provide a ready source of spilled grains intended for saddle animals.

Young are born in May, for a nest containing six small young, barely able to crawl, was found on May 20, and some other females trapped in this month were lactating. Numerous carnivorous animals prey upon rock squirrels, so it is understandable that four individuals ganged up in harassing a spotted skunk that was out during the day at Indian Garden.[14] It is surprising that as small a raptorial bird as

[14] *Ibid.*, no. 8 (1931): 82.

a sparrow hawk was successful in capturing and killing an adult rock squirrel, but such was the case at Hull Tank.[15]

Rock squirrels occur throughout the park, principally outside the coniferous forests. They are present from Havasu Canyon to Desert View, from Powell Plateau to Cape Royal, on the Tonto Plateau and along the Colorado River.

SPOTTED GROUND SQUIRREL
Spermophilus [Citellus] spilosoma

Description. A small ground squirrel with small white spots mottling the reddish-brown back and sides; tail not especially bushy and of about same color as back. Overall length, 7¼ to 9 inches (185 to 230 mm); tail, about 3¼ inches (85 mm); hind foot, about 1⅜ inches (35 mm).

Distribution. Arid, sandy parts of South Rim. Known only from western edge of park; possibly at southeastern corner also. See map, p. 97.

Habits. Spotted ground squirrels are desert inhabitants, preferring sandy, open terrain, and are closely associated with kangaroo rats and prairie dogs. Such habitat is available in the western part of the South Rim, for example, along Pasture Wash. The only specimens collected were from here, just south of Bass Camp. To the east, spotted ground squirrels almost reach the park boundary at Trash Tank. They apparently do not live in Havasu Canyon or on the Tonto Plateau.

Spotted ground squirrels are seed- and grass-eaters, are active only during the daytime, and hibernate during the colder parts of the winter in this part of Arizona.

[15] *Ibid.,* 7, no. 4 (1932): 40.

95

Spotted ground squirrel

WHITE-TAILED ANTELOPE SQUIRREL
Ammospermophilus [Citellus] leucurus

Description. A chipmunklike ground squirrel with a conspicuous white stripe not bordered with black on each side; underside of tail conspicuously white; otherwise upper parts are grayish brown. Overall length, 7¾ to 9 inches (195 to 230 mm); tail, 2½ to 3½ inches (60 to 85 mm); hind foot, about 1½ inches (38 mm).

Distribution. See map, p. 97.

Habits. These antelope ground squirrels are conspicuous, especially when they run, for they carry their broad, white tails curled over their backs. These squirrels are found in the open sagebrush of the western South Rim, from Pasture Wash westward to Hilltop, and on Great Thumb Point. Vernon Bailey reported them in Havasu Canyon also. They inhabit the blackbrush–greasebush–prickly pear–yucca association of the south Tonto Platform. Their burrows and the paths radiating out from them are unmistakable. The squirrels seem less shy there than at the top of the rim. Antelope squirrels live at a comparable elevation inside the canyon on the north side of the Colorado

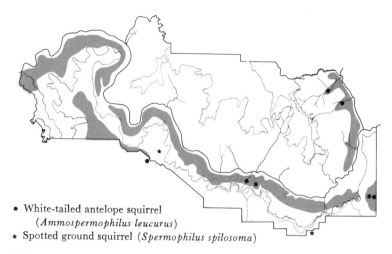

- White-tailed antelope squirrel
  (*Ammospermophilus leucurus*)
- ★ Spotted ground squirrel (*Spermophilus spilosoma*)

River, although their distribution there is not well known. These white-tails, common on the deserts to the east of the park, are also present along the eastern boundary of the park in the cactus–sagebrush–yucca association.

White-tails eat a variety of plant material and frequently climb into bushes in search of food. Near Hilltop we thought they were feeding on juniper berries. They eat cactus fruits and seeds, greasebush seeds, and many other kinds. These squirrels require some moisture, such as that obtained from most food items, for they cannot survive on metabolic water alone. Judging from when some of these squirrels were caught within the canyon, it is doubtful that they hibernate there.

White-tailed antelope squirrels gather seeds into their cheek pouches and then retire to their burrows to eat. When feeding on green vegetation, they remain at the food plants and away from the burrow for longer periods of time. Seeds of ephedra supplement those of yucca as food, and leaves of brome, galleta, and others are eaten as available.

Sometimes this ground squirrel and the next species, the golden-mantled ground squirrel, are mistakenly called chipmunks.

97

GOLDEN-MANTLED GROUND SQUIRREL
Spermophilus [Callospermophilus] lateralis

Description. A brightly colored, striped ground squirrel, sometimes mistakenly called a chipmunk, with a broad white stripe on each side, usually bordered with black, and a mantle on the shoulders of cinnamon to russet color, giving a "golden" appearance; the underside of the tail is brownish. Overall length, 9½ to 11½ inches (240 to 290 mm); tail, 3 to 4¼ inches (70 to 110 mm); hind foot, about 1½ inches (40 mm).

Distribution. See map, p. 99.

Habits. Golden-mantled ground squirrels are among the most conspicuous mammals on the North Rim — sunning on logs and rocks, sometimes giving their shrill whistle, often waiting for food to be offered. They are bold and adventuresome animals, for as soon as we left our tents during the day, golden-mantles came in to garner the cornmeal we had spilled. They feed on seeds, green leaves, and flowers and occasionally on animal matter, and by fall they have stored much fat which will be used during their hibernal inactivity. These squirrels can stuff much food in their cheek pouches.

Golden-mantled ground squirrels are coniferous and aspen forest inhabitants, yet rarely do they climb trees. Their nests are in burrows, often dug near a log, among roots, or under a boulder. They prefer moist woods and especially the edges of forests. These squirrels hiber-

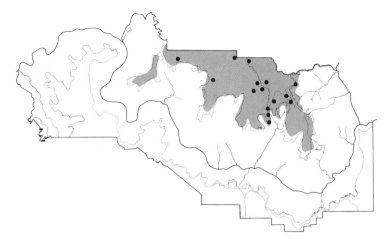

nate throughout the winter and are active for a relatively short time — mid-May to late September.

Adult squirrels undergo a summer molt from faded, worn to bright, fresh pelage in late June and July, with the subadults molting earliest.[16] An albino was seen at Tiyo Point and was not too conspicuous on the white rocks of the point.

Mantled ground squirrels are preyed upon by weasels, bobcats, foxes, coyotes, hawks, and snakes. Park naturalist Christiansen recorded a battle between a golden-mantled ground squirrel and a large gopher snake, with the squirrel successfully driving off the snake.

These ground squirrels have but one litter each year and the number of young per litter is usually between four and six. Many of the squirrels seen in late summer are young of the year. Only rarely do they emit a sharp, birdlike whistle.

[16] F. E. Durham, "Variation and Adaptations of the Rodents of the North Rim of the Grand Canyon, Arizona," in *Essays in Natural Science* (Los Angeles: University of Southern California Press, 1955), p. 237.

GUNNISON'S PRAIRIE DOG
Cynomys gunnisoni

Description. A thick-bodied, short-legged, short-tailed ground-dweller with small ears. Color, light reddish brown; tail with tip and underside whitish. Overall length, 13 to 14½ inches (325 to 365 mm); tail, 1¾ to 2¾ inches (45 to 68 mm); hind foot, about 2¼ inches (58 mm).

Distribution. On South Rim, western part at Pasture Wash (and only sometimes here).

Habits. Gunnison's prairie dogs inhabit the arid, level, high plateaus in open sagebrush or grassland, frequently at the edge of piñon-juniper forests. There is a limited amount of such habitat within the park. To the south, in Pasture Wash, there is suitable habitat and a small colony of prairie dogs which spills over into the park. As the "dogs" south of the park have been decimated several times by poisoning, so has the small portion of the colony within the park suffered. In 1942 and 1946 prairie dogs were numerous in Pasture Wash, in 1944 no occupied holes could be found, and in 1948 about fifteen were seen. In 1935 Natt Dodge recorded a large prairie dog town, covering at least three acres, about one-half mile east of the Berry Road and one-half mile south of the park boundary. In 1954 we saw old holes at Pasture Wash but no "dogs." However, in 1959 between eight and ten "dogs" were seen on April 28 and again on

May 21. This colony has fluctuated for many years. There is no reason why a dog town could not be maintained here if the part outside the park was not continuously decimated.

Gunnison's prairie dogs live in colonies or towns and dig sizable holes, with the dirt piled in a mound near the hole so it can be used as an elevated lookout post. Individuals give a sharp, loud bark, especially when alarmed. This "yip-yip" frequently betrays their presence long before they are seen. Prairie dogs are seed-eaters and as such are easily poisoned and represent a vanishing part of our western fauna.

Prairie dogs need open fields where they can follow the approach of possible predators. Well-worn paths converge on the mouth of the burrow entrance and serve as avenues of retreat as well as paths to search for seeds and leaves. Although these prairie dogs hibernate for parts of the winter, they may awaken and become active when snow still covers the ground.

Some prairie dogs have the tip of the tail blackish; others have it white. Gunnison's prairie dog has a white-tipped tail.

CLIFF CHIPMUNK
Eutamias dorsalis

Description. A rock- and cliff-dwelling chipmunk which is rusty or smoky gray with the stripes indistinct but often more obvious on the sides of the head than on the back; tail bushy and dark above, rusty-colored below. On the South Rim this is the only chipmunk. Overall length, 7¾ to 9 inches (195 to 225 mm); tail, 3⅜ to 4 inches (85 to 100 mm); hind foot, about 1¼ inches (32 mm).

Distribution.

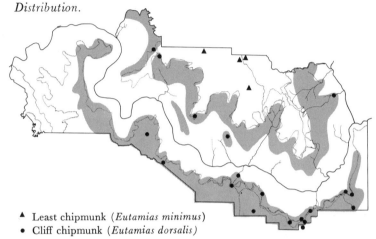

▲ Least chipmunk (*Eutamias minimus*)
● Cliff chipmunk (*Eutamias dorsalis*)

Habits. Cliff chipmunks prefer the rocks and cliffs, and thus are found not only along the edge of the South Rim but also down in the canyon, as at Indian Garden and Havasu Canyon. On the north side they are below the canyon rim. Cliff chipmunks are also present in the piñon-juniper belt on top of the South Rim where they readily feed on the piñon nuts. One animal was seen to put eleven piñon nuts in its check pouches and another animal that made its home in the women's dormitory at the village feasted on the girls' piñon nuts. As Abert squirrels buried piñon nuts, cliff chipmunks were seen to follow behind and dig them up.[17] They eat other seeds, fruits, and berries.

Young large enough to leave the nest have been seen by April 12 in the park. On November 6 they had not yet gone into hibernation, but this probably varies with the weather conditions of the year. Cliff chipmunks were active at the Village on December 10, 1950, when there was a warming of the weather, but their appearance was

[17] *Grand Canyon Nature Notes*, 4, no. 10 (1930): 65.

thought to be a break in their hibernation. Some were also seen at Bass Camp in February.

Cliff chipmunks can be quite vociferous, giving a sharp bark that is always accompanied by a twitch of the tail. One interested observer watching a chipmunk at a feeder in the Village recorded 172, 146, and 162 barks per minute for three different minutes and estimated this animal may have barked 5,800 times in a half hour.[18] And each with a twitch of the tail!

On the South Rim the numerous bird-feeders and eaves of houses have provided a ready source of food and shelter for cliff chipmunks, and their number has increased abnormally. For a while domestic cats preyed upon them, but when the cats were removed, they had even fewer enemies. They are also eaten by carnivorous mammals, hawks, and snakes.

LEAST CHIPMUNK
Eutamias minimus

Description. A small chipmunk with nine narrow stripes, five black and four whitish, on the back and sides; underside of the tail is yellowish. In contrast to the Uinta chipmunk, the least has the underparts washed with buff, the lateralmost dark stripe is obvious, and

[18] *Ibid.*, 2, no. 10 (1928): 1.

the sides are paler. Overall length, 7¼ to 8 inches (185 to 205 mm); tail, 3¼ to 3¾ inches (80 to 90 mm); hind foot, about 1¼ inches (31 mm).

Distribution. North Rim only. See map, p. 102.

Habits. Least chipmunks inhabit the more open parts of the coniferous forests and are not common throughout the North Rim. They do not hesitate to climb trees or bushes. They feed extensively on berries. Least chipmunks are not adverse to living in moist or wet places. Near the north entrance least and Uinta chipmunks can be found in the same area. In The Basin they were living in the tall grass and among the fallen trees.

UINTA CHIPMUNK
Eutamias umbrinus

Description. A large chipmunk with broad stripes on the back and white underparts. This is the large chipmunk of the North Rim forests. Can be distinguished from the least chipmunk by its larger size, white underparts, only a faint or no lateralmost dark stripe, and more reddish sides. Overall length, 8 to 9¼ inches (208 to 238 mm); tail, 3½ to 4¼ inches (85 to 105 mm); hind foot, about 1⅜ inches (34 mm).

Distribution. See map, p. 105.

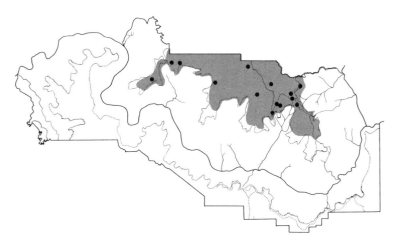

Habits. Uinta chipmunks are the tree-dwelling chipmunks of the campgrounds and many scenic spots of the North Rim. They often are found in association with golden-mantled ground squirrels. Uinta chipmunks prefer the yellow pine woodland, but at some places near the rim they live among piñon, juniper, and scrub oak.

Because of the great accumulation of snow on the North Rim where both Uinta and least chipmunks live, it is essential that they hibernate for long periods of the winter. Therefore, much fat must be accumulated during the summer to be used in this winter sleep.

Young must be born in early July, for some specimens taken in early August were about two-thirds grown. No females taken in August were nursing young so these juveniles were on their own. They had not yet molted into adult pelage.

Uinta chipmunks were formerly confused with the species known as the Colorado chipmunk (*Eutamias quadrivittatus*). In Nevada the preferred habitat of the Uinta chipmunk is among the yellow and white pines. Some occur among the thick stands of aspen.

Within the park there are three kinds of chipmunks and the golden-mantled ground squirrel, which might be confused with the chipmunks. On the South Rim there is only the cliff chipmunk. On the North Rim there are the cliff chipmunk, Uinta chipmunk, least chipmunk, and the golden-mantled ground squirrel. On the rocky edges of the North Rim the cliff chipmunk is present. In the pines there are Uinta chipmunks and golden-mantled ground squirrels. Least chipmunks are more restricted to grassy areas within the forests.

ABERT SQUIRREL
Sciurus aberti

Description. A large, bushy-eared tree squirrel with the head, most of back and sides, and top of tail gray, almost bluish gray; middle of back reddish; underparts, including underside of tail, white; sides with a blackish band where gray meets white; gray on top of tail bordered with white. Ears with tufts or tassels (these are sometimes called "tufted-eared" or "tassel-eared" squirrels); tufts often inconspicuous or lost during summer. Overall length, 19 to 21 inches (480 to 535 mm); tail, 7¼ to 9¾ inches (185 to 245 mm); hind foot, 2¾ to 3⅛ inches (67 to 78 mm); ear, about 1¾ inches (44 mm); tassels may extend ¾ inch beyond tip of ear.

Distribution. South Rim only. See map, p. 109.

Habits. The tree-dwelling squirrel of the South Rim is the Abert or tufted-eared squirrel. It is an inhabitant of mature yellow or ponderosa pines but on occasion lives in piñons and junipers. Seven of twelve nests studied in the park were in yellow pine and five in piñon.[19] Abert squirrels rarely become accustomed to man as do rock squirrels and chipmunks and thus are not as readily seen. However, sometimes they will come to bird-feeders.

Nests are placed well up in pines and are about 12 inches in diameter, with two tunnels leading into an inner chamber which is

[19] *Ibid.,* no. 8 (1928): 1.

about 5 inches in diameter. The entire structure is built on a founda-
tion of twigs, 8 to 12 inches long, placed in a crotch. Bark is used
in the nest, with the shredded parts forming the inner chamber. The
nest is kept in a constant state of repair.[20] In late winter or early
spring squirrels will often be seen with a mouthful of shredded juniper bark to be added to the inner nest. Mating takes place in late
February and March. During this time squirrels are more active than
usual, chasing one another. Young, usually numbering four, are born
in these nests in late March or early April. Mothers have been seen
transporting their young as late as May 13. They do this by picking
up each young in the mouth. By late June young of the year are feeding among the pines.

Abert squirrels feed extensively on the seeds of the yellow or ponderosa pine but in the park on piñon nuts as well. Pine cones are
cut, carried to a safe feeding spot in the tree, the scales removed,
and the nutlets beneath each scale eaten. Or seeds that have fallen
to the ground may be gleaned and eaten. They also feed on mistletoe
and the inner bark of the pine. Apparently little or no food is stored
in the nests but squirrels cache seeds in the ground for later needs.
These squirrels do not hibernate and, although not as active during
the coldest days, feed and forage throughout the winter. Often they
can be seen in winter digging up buried seeds at the snow-free bases
of trees or eating the smaller twigs of the yellow pine. Ranger Brooks
records a conflict between an Abert squirrel and two ravens over a
supply of piñon nuts. Eventually the squirrel prevailed, using a rush-
ing and bumping technique to drive the birds away.[21]

Abert squirrels are white-bellied in contrast to the black-bellied
Kaibab squirrel. However, a few Aberts have black bellies. When a
sizable number of Aberts is examined, usually at least one is black
below. However, none of these has the conspicuous white tail of the
Kaibab, retaining the gray-topped tail, although one had numerous
white hairs interspersed with the gray. Only two Kaibab squirrels are
known to have reverted back to the white-belly coloration of the
Abert squirrel, according to Dr. Joseph Hall, an authority on these

[20] *Ibid.*
[21] *Ibid.*, 8, no. 11 (1934): 247.

squirrels. These two have the white tails of typical Kaibabs. It thus appears that the white color of the underparts most often mutates to black, rarely the black to white. The color of the tail mutates least of all.

Cars, hawks, and disease are probably the main decimating factors of the Abert squirrels. When car speeds within the park were greatly reduced, as during World War II, there was an increase in Abert squirrels, but when speeds increased, fewer squirrels were evident. Dr. Harold Bryant, former park superintendent, related that six were killed along one block of the Village during a short period. Outside the park there is an established hunting season for Abert squirrels, and many are harvested each fall in northern Arizona.

On the North Rim the Kaibab squirrel, which is very much like the Abert, occupies a similar niche in the yellow pine forest. It has been conjectured that a population, perhaps small, of Aberts got across the gorge and the river and invaded the North Rim. In all likelihood, this would have been during the late Pleistocene. There, in the isolation of the yellow pine forest, a distinctive population of squirrels evolved which are known as Kaibab squirrels. Abert and Kaibab squirrels have not greatly differentiated.

Abert squirrels have a restricted distribution in Colorado, Utah, Arizona, and New Mexico southward along the Sierra Occidental into Mexico. There they are to be found as far south as the state of Durango.

KAIBAB SQUIRREL
Sciurus kaibabensis

Description. A large tree squirrel of the same color and size as the Abert squirrel *except* top of tail as well as bottom white and the underparts black or dark gray. Lengths as for Abert squirrel.

Distribution.

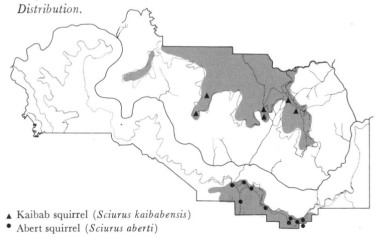

▲ Kaibab squirrel (*Sciurus kaibabensis*)
● Abert squirrel (*Sciurus aberti*)

Habits. The Kaibab squirrel is the most unique mammal of Grand Canyon, for here and a short distance to the north is its entire range.

109

This North Rim counterpart of the Abert squirrel is similar to it in nearly all respects, including ear tufts, except the tail is almost white and the underparts are black or dark gray. For some reason, not obvious, the Kaibab squirrel is much more shy than the Abert and is not frequently seen. Many times a person will walk under a tree where a Kaibab squirrel has remained silent, far up in the tree, without ever knowing it was there. Usually their silhouettes must be detected, for their activities and chatter will not betray them.

Because of more severe winters on the North Rim, mating and birth of young are delayed about three months over those of the Abert squirrel. Young are not born until late June or July and average four per litter. The nest is similar to that of the Abert squirrel, placed well up in a yellow pine, but some nests have only one entranceway. Ranger-naturalist Ralph Redburn studied the development of five young Kaibabs by climbing to the nest and examining the growing young. On July 2 the five did not have their eyes opened, nor did they on the next seven days. On July 10 the eyes were open and the young gave faint squeaks. By July 20 the young had rapidly developed and were cautiously navigating the branches. The hair on the body and tail was short but the ear tufts were already apparent.[22] Dr. Joseph Hall examined young in a nest 35 feet up in a yellow pine at the North Rim Campground. On June 26 they were judged to be two days old, pink and naked with the eyes unopened, each about $3\frac{1}{2}$ inches from nose to tip of tail and weighing about 9 grams ($\frac{3}{10}$ ounce). By August 21, eight weeks later, the now half-grown young were playing in the branches and on the ground. During those eight weeks the mother moved the young two times because of disturbances by humans.

Kaibab squirrels feed primarily on yellow pine seeds and inner bark. In the winter, when seeds are not available and the snow is deep, a squirrel cuts off the terminal part of a small yellow pine branch and then cuts off and discards the part with the needles. The gray outer bark is stripped off with the teeth and the red inner bark is eaten.[23] In summer squirrels frequently eat mushrooms, especially

[22] *Ibid.*, 7, no. 7 (1932): 66-68.
[23] Joseph G. Hall, "White Tails and Yellow Pines," *National Park Magazine*, 41, no. 235 (1967): 9-11.

those that grow just below the surface of the pine duff. In 1942 a pair that nested near the campground reportedly entered the cafeteria kitchen for food, thus overcoming their shyness. These squirrels do not hibernate during the winter, and the rangers stationed at the North Rim Bright Angel Ranger Station during the winter in 1930-31 found that two pairs of Kaibab squirrels readily came to the feeder outside a window.

Numbers of Kaibab squirrels seem to fluctuate. In 1928 they reportedly were "plentiful"; in 1932 someone guessed there might be 120 individuals within the park, but this estimate was probably low; in 1947 naturalist Christiansen reported seeing only twelve during the entire summer. In about one week in 1954 we saw six. Although the numbers fluctuate, there are far fewer individuals in the park now than in some earlier years. As Joseph Hall so aptly put it, "The welfare of the forests of ponderosa pine is the welfare of this squirrel."[24]

Although search has been made for Kaibab squirrels in the yellow pine forests of Shiva Temple, none was found. Kaibab squirrels have been seen on Powell Plateau but no specimens have been collected there.

A study made in 1966 by the Arizona Game and Fish Department of Kaibab squirrels outside the park indicated that there were six squirrels per roadside mile. This information was based on tracks in the snow, clippings from feeding activities, and observations of animals. The department has marked and released some Kaibab squirrels in an attempt to learn more about their life history.

The Kaibab squirrel is included in the 1966 list of "Rare and endangered fish and wildlife of the United States."

[24] *Ibid.*

RED SQUIRREL, CHICKAREE
Tamiasciurus hudsonicus

Description. A small tree squirrel, dark gray in color, but with a rusty tinge, with white underparts and a narrow black stripe on the sides where the gray meets the white; tail above and below slightly darker than the back with some white hairs along the edge. Ears not tasseled and small. Overall length, 12½ to 14 inches (320 to 350 mm); tail, 4¾ to 6¼ inches (120 to 160 mm); hind foot, 1¾ to 2¼ inches (45 to 55 mm); ear, about 1⅛ inches (28 mm).

Distribution. See map, p. 113.

Habits. The noise-makers of the North Rim are the red squirrels, also called chickarees or spruce squirrels. At the slightest provocation they will give their oft-repeated call of "chr-r-r-, che-e-e-e," and only when danger gets too close will they fall silent. These squirrels prefer the spruce and fir belt and usually are above the yellow pine zone. Because of this, they are often given the common name of spruce squirrels. However, on occasion they have been known to drive Kaibab squirrels out of their favorite trees in the yellow pines. Red squirrels commonly build their nests in the abandoned holes made by woodpeckers. Often they construct ball-shaped nests, about a foot in diameter, out of twigs, bark, and leaves. These are placed out on a branch, several feet from the trunk, and well up in the tree. These

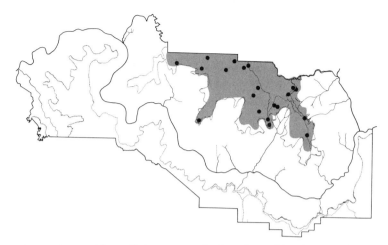

nests must provide sufficient warmth for the cold winters of the North Rim. Red squirrels are not known to hibernate.

Food consists principally of the seeds of conifers, supplemented with mushrooms, buds, fruit, and other seeds. These squirrels feed on the cones while sitting high in the tree near the trunk by clipping off the scales, one by one, and then discarding the core. This accounts for the accumulation of quantities of scales and cores under some trees — as much as fifteen bushels under some trees from several generations of squirrels. Many cones are cached beneath the tree or in the cone scale heap where they will be available for winter food. Apparently, red squirrels recognize those cones which have mature, ripe seeds and cut only those.

Young must be born in late April or early May. Young of the year which were nearly adult-size were collected during the first week of August. Females may produce two litters during the summer, for two animals were found to be nursing young during the second week of August. An albinistic red squirrel was seen at Robbers Roost in 1936 and 1938. If this was the same individual, it survived three seasons in spite of its abnormal color.

POCKET GOPHERS (Family Geomyidae)

Pocket gophers are burrowing rodents that spend their lifetime below ground. They have strong incisor teeth and long claws on the front feet for digging, fur-lined cheek pouches, small eyes, and a nearly naked but highly sensitive tail. The tail acts as a "feeler" to aid the gopher in running rapidly backward through its underground burrows. Where the burrow is extended to the surface, a mound of dirt is thrown up. Normally a gopher plugs its burrow opening so that no hole is visible; a ground squirrel's burrow is open.

There are two species of pocket gophers in the park. One, the northern pocket gopher, is restricted to the North Rim. Since both are so similar, their habits are discussed in one account below.

*Common
pocket gopher*

Northern pocket gopher

COMMON POCKET GOPHER
Thomomys bottae

Description. A medium-sized pocket gopher with small ears, forefeet with well-clawed toes, nearly hairless tail, and prominent cheek pouches (hence the name). Pouches usually lined with white fur and sides of animal reddish. Overall length, 6¾ to 9½ inches (170 to 240 mm); tail, 2 to 2¾ inches (50 to 70 mm); hind foot, 1 to 1¾ inches (25 to 34 mm).

NORTHERN POCKET GOPHER
Thomomys talpoides

Description. A medium-sized pocket gopher, essentially the same as the common pocket gopher, but distinguishable by more prominent white markings under chin, cheek pouches usually lined with black fur, tan-colored sides, more conspicuous black patch behind each ear, and by the absence of the sphenoidal fissure on the side of the cranium (present in *T. bottae*).

Distribution.

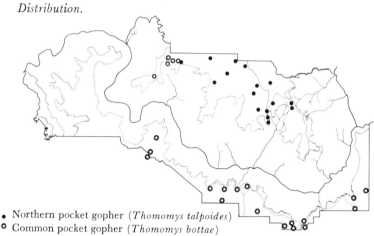

• Northern pocket gopher (*Thomomys talpoides*)
○ Common pocket gopher (*Thomomys bottae*)

Habits. Common pocket gophers are found on the South Rim and the warmer west end of the North Rim; northern pocket gophers live in the mountain meadows of the North Rim. The presence of pocket gophers is readily made known not by the animals themselves but by their characteristic gopher mounds. The pile of dirt at the mouth of a tunnel which has been brought to the surface from their underground mining operations forms a cone or mound of soil. One gopher will produce many such mounds where he has pushed out the dirt from the deeper tunnel. It is not possible to say how many mounds are made by one animal, but mounds of fresh dirt indicate belowground activity. Rarely is the tunnel entrance left open for any period of time but, rather, it is plugged with dirt to keep out the wind and

115

especially such predators as weasels and snakes. A weasel was caught in a trap set specifically for a gopher at The Basin on the North Rim. Badgers will dig gophers out; other predators will take them at their burrow entrances. Gophers spend nearly all their time within these subterranean runways and rarely move about on the surface, although we did catch two in rat traps on the surface.

Food consists principally of roots. Tunnels are dug to the base of a plant with a tuberous root and part or all of the root may be eaten — even the leafy part of the plant may be pulled below the surface and the stem, leaves, and seeds eaten. When a heavy blanket of snow covers the ground, gophers will forage for surface vegetation by tunneling through the snow but on the surface of the ground. Usually, soil is pushed into these snow tunnels and when the snow melts, a network of earthen cores remains on the surface of the ground.

Pocket gophers are usually solitary, one to a network of tunnels, except during the short mating season. Common pocket gophers had embryos, near full term, on July 4 and young one-third grown on August 8. Northern pocket gophers had young one-third to half grown by mid-August. In all likelihood, females have more than one litter per year.

Within the park pocket gophers live in a variety of soils, from deep friable soil to shallow rocky soil. It is imperative that the ground be adequately drained, without prolonged periods of standing water. There apparently is not adequate soil or food at Indian Garden or Phantom Ranch. Nests and food caches are placed in parts of the burrow system that afford the best chances of continued dryness.

POCKET MICE AND KANGAROO RATS
(Family Heteromyidae)

These are small- to medium-sized mice which are specialized for jumping with small front legs and feet, long hind legs and feet, and long tails, usually bushy near the tip. They are especially adapted to living in desert conditions, being able to subsist with a minimum of drinking water.

Silky pocket mouse

Rock pocket mouse

SILKY POCKET MOUSE
Perognathus flavus

Description. A small jumping mouse with relatively large hind feet and eyes. Fur buff-colored and silky with the color of the underparts whitish; lighter-colored patch of fur immediately behind ear. Tail thinly haired and about equal to length of head and body. Overall length, 4⅛ to 4¾ inches (105 to 120 mm); tail, 2 to 2½ inches (48 to 62 mm); hind foot, about ¾ inch (17 mm).

Distribution.

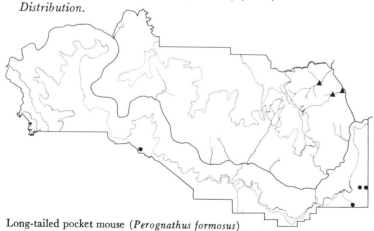

▲ Long-tailed pocket mouse (*Perognathus formosus*)
● Silky pocket mouse (*Perognathus flavus*)

117

Habits. Silky pocket mice are the smallest rodents in the park, being slightly smaller than harvest mice. They are desert-dwellers, preferring sandy soil in which they dig burrows. The burrows are small in diameter and the entrances are usually plugged during the day. This provides protection from enemies and from hot, desiccating winds. Near Cedar Mountain silky pocket mice were caught in the sagebrush-cactus association below the junipers. At Pasture Wash one was taken along the dirt road in the sagebrush. At both places silky pocket mice were probably living in a situation that was not ideal for this species, and this accounts for the few taken. In most places silky pocket mice prefer open desert conditions where there is sparse, widely scattered vegetation. They are shy animals and often avoid strange objects, such as traps that will catch them.

These pocket mice are primarily seed-eaters. Seeds are temporarily stored in the cheek pouches for transfer to cache sites in an underground burrow.

ROCK POCKET MOUSE
Perognathus intermedius

Description. A medium-sized jumping mouse with a bushy tail and spinelike hairs which project beyond the fur on the rump. Tail decidedly longer than the body. Color of upper parts yellowish gray with an intermingling of black hairs. Overall length, 6 to 7 inches (155 to 175 mm); tail, 3⅜ to 4 inches (85 to 100 mm); hind foot, about 1 inch (23 mm).

Distribution. See map, p. 119.

Habits. These nocturnal pocket mice prefer the rockiest slopes, almost cliffs, in which to live. Therefore, it is little wonder that they are common from Hilltop and Bass Camp to the Tonto Plateau. Rock pocket mice also live within the Inner Gorge of the canyon but only on the south side. Some have been taken at the base of the cliffs of the gorge's south face. Although rock pocket mice prefer slopes, some mice live on level, sandy ground among blackbrush and greasebush on the Tonto Plateau in a situation where one would not expect them. Perhaps they have moved out, through population pressure, from the nearby rocky walls. In contrast, at Hilltop rock pocket

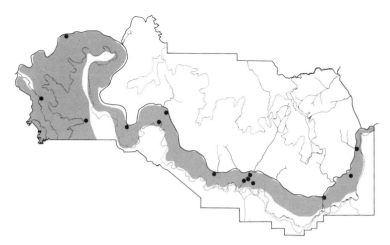

mice were taken only from the steep sides of rocky ravines with very little vegetation.

When Vernon Bailey explored the lower parts of the Tanner Trail one summer, he opened the burrow of a rock pocket mouse. The temperature at the bottom of its burrow at 9 A.M. was a cool 82° F; on the previous day the ground-level temperature was 144° F. The burrow was only a little over a foot below the surface but this insulation was effective.

Breeding is underway in late April, for a female collected on May 10 contained five embryos. In all likelihood, it starts even earlier than this. Half-grown young are abroad by the middle of July. It is not clear if females have more than one litter each year or if they hibernate in mid-winter. Rock pocket mice are preyed upon by owls, snakes, ringtails, and other carnivorous mammals.

LONG-TAILED POCKET MOUSE
Perognathus formosus

Description. A medium-sized, dark-colored jumping mouse with a conspicuously bushy tail but without spinelike hairs on the rump. Color of upper parts blackish with intermingled brownish hairs; underparts white with a frosting of yellow; tail above and below about the same color as the upper parts and underparts respectively. Body length in long-tailed pocket mice usually 80 mm or more; in rock pocket mice, usually less than 80 mm. Overall length, 7 to 8 inches (180 to 202 mm); tail, about 4 inches (100 to 112 mm); hind foot, about 1 inch (23 to 25 mm).

Distribution. North side of Colorado River; known only from along and near the mouth of Kwagunt Creek and in Nankoweap Canyon at the east and Deer Creek Falls at the west. See map, p. 117.

Habits. Long-tailed pocket mice have a limited range and are poorly known within the park and were not taken there until 1969. Their distribution in the sandy washes leading into the Colorado River may be extensive since most of these have not been investigated. The specimen from along Kwagunt Creek, two miles above its mouth, was taken in the rocky riverbed in rocks and hard-packed sand. There were a few mesquites and junipers but little other vegetation. At the mouth of Kwagunt Creek the mice were taken on sandy soil in a thicket of open mesquite. Some grasses were present, and one of these was probably Indian rice-grass, *Oryzopsis.* The sand was not so hard-packed here but that numerous rodent tracks were evident in the early morning. Elsewhere long-tailed pocket mice are known to prefer rocky ground, with the rocks up to several inches in diameter. This is more like the habitat in Nankoweap Canyon where they live in soil packed with marble-sized pebbles among blackbrush, ephedra, and cacti. Often they live at the bottom of talus slopes or cliffs. The presence of these pocket mice is often made known by small cascades of dirt or sand, like miniature taluses, at the base of rocks. Seemingly suitable habitat is present along the Colorado River in Grand Canyon, but long-tailed pocket mice have previously been taken no closer than the lower end of Toroweap Valley to the west and House Rock Valley to the north.

ORD'S KANGAROO RAT
Dipodomys ordii

Description. A large jumping mouse (or a small jumping rat) with an exceedingly long tail. Color of upper parts buffy yellow, underparts white; conspicuous white patch behind each ear and white stripe over each hip. Hind feet long and white. Tail with lateral white stripes, being brownish above and below; tail well haired at end. Overall length, 9 to 10 inches (225 to 255 mm); tail, 5¼ to 6 inches (130 to 148 mm); hind foot, about 1½ inches (40 mm).

Distribution. On South Rim, western part at Pasture Wash, and nearly entering the eastern part, as near Trash Tank.

Habits. Kangaroo rats are open desert inhabitants where there is soil suitable for digging burrows. Apparently such habitat is available only at Pasture Wash, where Gunnison's prairie dogs and silky pocket mice also live. The habitat at Pasture Wash must barely meet the requirements of the Ord's kangaroo rat, for several of the animals we caught were juveniles, and we thought the young might have been forced into this area by greater population pressure to the south.

Since these kangaroo rats are nocturnal, they frequently are seen at night in a headlight or flashlight beam as these long-tailed rats move around in search of seeds. They are clean animals, especially if dust is available in which they can "bathe." Numerous persons have been successful in making attractive pets of kangaroo rats.

We have no reason to believe that Ord's kangaroo rats live within the canyon. However, E. D. McKee found some holes "in the large sand dune areas south of the Colorado opposite Tapeats Creek" on November 12, 1937, that he thought might have been made by these animals. Further investigations are necessary.

BEAVERS (Family Castoridae)

Beavers are large rodents that are specialized for living in water. The tail is broad and flattened like a paddle, the hind feet are webbed, and the fur is luxuriant and dense.

BEAVER
Castor canadensis

Description. Grand Canyon beavers are light-colored with the fur of the back yellowish-cinnamon color; otherwise the characters are those given for the family. Overall length, 40 to 48 inches (1,000 to 1,200 mm); tail, 15 to 21 inches (390 to 530 mm); hind foot, 6¾ to 7½ inches (170 to 190 mm).

Distribution. Tributaries of the Colorado River, especially Bright Angel Creek (see below for records).

Habits. Beavers have lived along the Colorado River and in its tributaries within the park boundaries for a long time. Perhaps their successful existence was due to the inaccessibility of their abode to early fur trappers. Fur hunters as early as 1826 did remove beaver from the park area, but the difficulty in obtaining them did not appeal to the trappers.

The principal source of food for beavers within the canyon is the cottonwood, and since this is such a fast-growing tree, they have not eaten themselves out of home. They feed on the leaves and the bark, which they handily strip from the limbs with their long incisors. Trees up to a foot in diameter are readily felled in the canyon. If cottonwood is not immediately available, beaver will turn to cutting and eating tamarix, willow, and mesquite. Since some flooding along the Colorado River has been controlled by the establishment of the Glen Canyon dam, cottonwoods, tamarix, and willows may become more plentiful along this river. In turn, this may permit the establishment of more beaver. One hardly expects to find beaver feeding on desert mesquite growing on the sandy beaches of the Colorado. But such is the case. We found their footprints and the unmistakable groove of their broad tails where they had trudged through the soft, hot sand to clumps of mesquite. Here they had cut the small branches and fed on the bark of the mesquite. And during the night, when beavers do most of their feeding, the temperature had not dropped much below 90° F.

Beavers build dams on many of the tributary creeks of the Colorado, such as Bright Angel, Phantom, Kwagunt, and others. Along most of the shores of the Colorado River there is not suitable cover or food. Through the summer and fall beavers work assiduously to build their dams, and nearly every spring, with heavy rains and melting snow, these are washed out.

Some of the places where beaver are now or have been known, as these are recorded primarily in the files of the Grand Canyon Museum, are: along and near mouth of Bright Angel Creek; Phantom Ranch; just above Phantom Ranch; Cottonwood Camp; 1 mile above Cottonwood Camp; 6 miles north of Phantom Ranch; 2 miles south of Ribbon Falls; along Kwagunt Creek; mouth of and along Wall Creek; Colorado River opposite Deer Creek Falls; mouth of Whitman Wash; Chuar Creek; Colorado River at Mile 193; Colorado River at Mile 196; between Nankoweap and Kwagunt; along Colorado River, ¾ mile west of mouth of Parashont Canyon; along river below Spencer Canyon; Havasu Canyon just above Beaver Falls; Colorado River, 2 miles and 5 miles south of mouth of Little Colorado River. In 1913 Edward Goldman of the United States Biological Surveys found them along Indian Garden Creek and in 1889 Vernon Bailey found them along the Little Colorado at Cameron.

In some places beavers construct both a lodge within their dam and a bank den. The latter is less affected by floods. Bank dens have an underwater entrance and a short burrow opening into a small chamber, seldom exceeding 3 feet in diameter.[25] The nest within the lodge or the chamber is built above the high-water level so that the nest stays dry. The den is often made of willow, arrow wood, and cottonwood. It is not known when young beavers are born in the canyon nor how many there are in a litter.

NEW WORLD RATS AND MICE (Family Cricetidae)

Grasshopper mice, harvest mice, various species of *Peromyscus* (sometimes given the collective name of white-footed mice), wood rats, cotton rats, and voles (meadow mice) are in this family. These are small- to medium-sized rodents with conspicuous ears, light underparts, and tail often about as long as the body, sometimes longer. Although some of these mice and rats are quite like the house mouse and the barn rat, they are not closely related, for the latter are introductions from the Old World.

[25] C. Markley, *Grand Canyon Nature Notes*, 5, no. 8 (1931): 78-80.

SHORT-TAILED OR NORTHERN GRASSHOPPER MOUSE
Onychomys leucogaster

Description. A short-tailed, plump-bodied mouse that is brownish gray although juveniles are more nearly lead gray; underparts white. Tail so short that it is only half or less the length of the head and body. Overall length, 5¾ to 6¼ inches (144 to 160 mm); tail, 1½ to 2⅛ inches (35 to 55 mm); hind foot, about 1 inch (22 mm).

Distribution. South Rim only: in western part near Pasture Wash, centrally at Hermit Basin, and in eastern part near Cedar Mountain.

Habits. Grasshopper mice feed so extensively on insects, including grasshoppers, that this is the basis for their name. One study indicates that 79 per cent of their food, based on stomach analysis, is insects. The stomach of one specimen caught by us at Pasture Wash contained only insects, and these were mainly coleopteran beetles. We caught one grasshopper mouse in a trap during the middle of the day in mid-July. One wonders if it might have been foraging for insects and fallen prey to our traps since the bait on our traps often attracted insects. These mice also eat some seeds and green vegetation.

Grasshopper mice either dig their own burrows or use the burrows of other mice, kangaroo rats, or even pocket gophers. These mice have an interesting habit of making a shrill, very high whistle which is of short duration but audible for some distance. In captivity they stand upright on their hind feet and slightly elevate their heads when they make this sound.

Our specimens were taken in sagebrush flats and in thickets of sage-brush and cactus. Probably the Tonto Platform is too low zonally for northern grasshopper mice, but continued search for them should be made there.

WESTERN HARVEST MOUSE
Reithrodontomys megalotis

Description. A small-bodied, reddish-brown mouse with a long tail. In size, much like the common house mouse, but color more brownish, underparts whitish or silvery, and front face of each upper incisor with a lengthwise groove. Overall length, 5 to 6 inches (125 to 150 mm); tail, 2½ to 3 inches (60 to 72 mm); hind foot, about ⅝ inch (16 mm).

Distribution. See map, p. 127.

Habits. Harvest mice must be nearly as ubiquitous as deer mice within the park, for they live from hot, deserty conditions at the mouth of Bright Angel Creek to the cool boreal forests of Fuller Canyon on the North Rim — from 2,500 feet to 8,500 feet in an air-line distance of 10 miles. These small nocturnal mice often live in grassy places and may use the runways of meadow voles. Elsewhere they live in thickets of tumbleweed and at night may be found up in the dry bushes harvesting the seed. Near Cedar Mountain they were found in sagebrush and cactus.

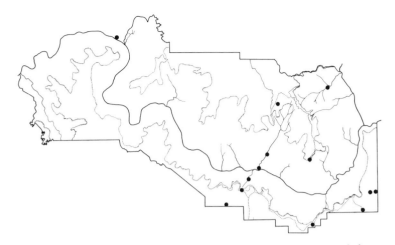

One female collected on June 23 was lactating yet carried four small embryos. Obviously she was going to have at least two litters. In Nevada harvest mice were found to be pregnant in the months of May through August.[26] These mice are primarily seed-eaters. Probably nearly every small predatory mammal, many predatory birds, and snakes feed on these harvest mice.

DEER MOUSE
Peromyscus maniculatus

Description. A small peromyscine with the shortest tail of any of the five kinds in the park; tail rarely more than 3 inches long and with a narrow, dark, dorsal stripe. Ears short and with a fine edging of white. All peromyscines in the park have white feet (often called white-footed mice), whitish underparts including whitish underside of tail, and large eyes; the young are gray. Differences between the species are principally in size of ears, length of tail, hairiness of tail, and overall size. Deer mice are reddish brown or yellowish brown in color. Overall length, 5¾ to 7 inches (148 to 178 mm); tail, 2¼ to 3¼ inches (55 to 84 mm); hind foot, about ¾ inch (19 to 22 mm); ear, about ¾ inch (18 mm).

[26] E. R. Hall, *Mammals of Nevada* (Berkeley and Los Angeles: University of California Press, 1946).

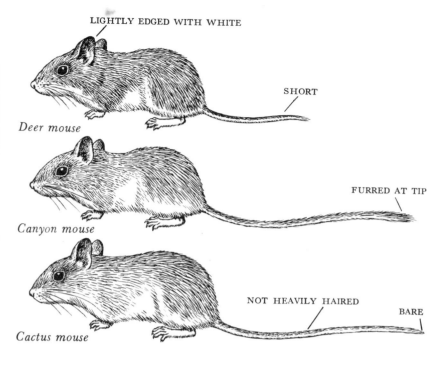

SMALL-EARED, SMALL- TO MEDIUM-SIZED BODY

LIGHTLY EDGED WITH WHITE

SHORT

Deer mouse

FURRED AT TIP

Canyon mouse

NOT HEAVILY HAIRED

BARE

Cactus mouse

LARGE-EARED, LARGE BODY

SHORTER THAN HIND FOOT

LONGER THAN BODY

Brush mouse

LONGER THAN HIND FOOT

SHORTER THAN BODY

Piñon mouse

Five species of Peromyscus *in the park. (When comparing features, note the relative size of the body and the length of the tail.)*

Distribution.

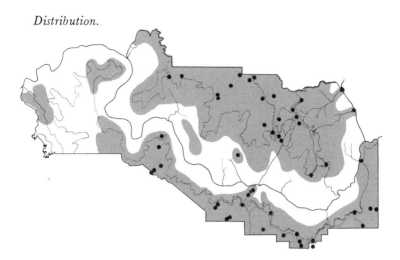

Habits. Deer mice live in a great variety of places — in the cool coniferous forests of the North Rim to the cacti of Cedar Mountain, from Shiva Temple to the cottages at the Village. They build their nests under or in logs, in crevices in rocks, in piles of sticks or cacti, or in drawers and cupboards. On the rims they are nearly everywhere, but few are found deep down in the canyon. Here they are replaced by cactus mice. Only a few deer mice have been taken around Indian Garden and on the Tonto Plateau, but many cactus mice have. Deer mice are especially uncommon in the Inner Gorge and along the Colorado River for only a few specimens have been taken there and at only three localities.

Probably deer mice have several litters of young each year. In all of the summer months that we collected them, at least some females were pregnant. Deer mice are omnivorous but prefer seeds. Like all mammals, deer mice have home ranges or home regions where most of their activities are carried on. There is some evidence to indicate that, for these deer mice, the home range varies between a quarter and a half acre. Deer mice serve as an important food item for most predaceous animals, and in turn these predators serve to prevent an overabundance of deer mice.

BRUSH MOUSE
Peromyscus boylii

Description. A large peromyscine with a long tail that is usually longer than the head and body. Ears large but *shorter* than the hind feet. Tail sufficiently sparsely haired that annulations of skin visible. Upper parts brownish. Overall length, 7¼ to 8¼ inches (185 to 212 mm); hind foot, about ⅞ inch (22 mm); ear, about ¾ inch (19 mm).

Distribution.

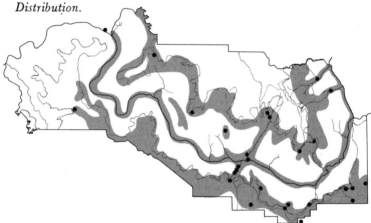

Habits. Brush mice are the most cosmopolitan of the white-footed mice in the park. They have been taken at Phantom Ranch, at 2,300 feet along the Colorado River at the mouth of Bright Angel Creek, at 7,900 feet at Cape Final, and from the westernmost to the easternmost boundaries of the park on the rims. They are present on Shiva Temple and probably on many other buttes within the canyon. They live in nearly as wide a variety of places as do harvest mice. Brush mice frequent the piñon-juniper flats, the cottonwood-willow association, the rocky slopes, and brushy-weedy situations. They may be associated with any of the other species of white-footed mice but do not readily live in the spruce-fir forests of the North Rim.

Females have more than one litter each year. One taken in August was nursing young and was about to have another brood. One kept by

Vernon Bailey gave birth to four young on May 2. The home ranges in some populations of brush mice may be as small as a quarter acre.

Brush mice feed on nuts, acorns, seeds, berries, insects, and occasionally green vegetation. They do not store food nor do they hibernate.

PIÑON MOUSE
Peromyscus truei

Description. A large peromyscine with especially large ears that are longer than the hind feet. Tail *shorter* than the head and body and usually less than 100 mm; tail well haired, nearly concealing the annulations, and with a noticeable terminal tuft. Upper parts dark brown. Overall length, 7 to 8 inches (175 to 205 mm); tail, 3⅜ to 4 inches (83 to 102 mm); hind foot, about ⅞ inch (23 mm); ear, about 1 inch (25 mm).

Distribution.

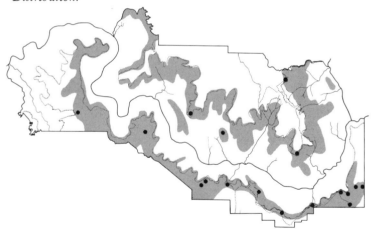

Habits. Piñon mice live in rocky areas where there are piñon trees. Both items are a requisite, for usually piñons without rocks or rocks without piñons will not provide suitable habitat. Because this habitat is often found on sunny cliffs, these mice are sometimes called cliff mice. The pine-covered cliffs of the canyon are no barrier to these mice, and therefore their presence on the buttes within the canyon that support piñon trees is to be expected. Such is the case on Shiva Temple. Often the piñons are in association with cliff rose and fernbush.

Piñon mice feed extensively on piñon nuts and frequently climb the trees in seeking food; traps set in these trees may catch the mice.

CANYON MOUSE
Peromyscus crinitus

Description. A small-bodied, short-eared peromyscine. The tail is well furred, has a noticeable terminal tuft, and is longer than the head and body. Pelage long, lax, and mottled yellowish brown or buffy; frequently a spot of yellowish fur between the forelegs; otherwise whitish underparts. Overall length, 6½ to 7¼ inches (160 to 185 mm); tail, 3½ to 4 inches (85 to 105 mm); hind foot, about ¾ inch (19 mm); ear, about ¾ inch (19 mm).

Distribution.

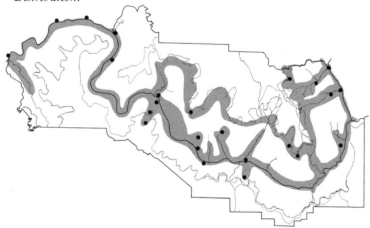

Habits. Canyon mice are inhabitants of the rocky, nearly barren canyon walls, whether such rocky places are at 8,800 feet as at Point Imperial or at 2,500 feet along the rocky canyon sides at the mouth of Bright Angel Creek. Canyon mice are probably abundant and widespread on many of the canyon walls where it is impossible for man to study them. They are present on Shiva Temple and perhaps the other buttes within the canyon. Specimens are known from few localities on the South Rim: vicinity of Bass Camp, Supai Canyon, Yavapai Point Trail, mouth of Hermit Creek, and Pipe Creek. Canyon mice do not live on rocky slopes that are wooded. Some did live in the rock fences near the cliffs at Phantom Ranch. They probably harvested the grain which is spilled in the mule corrals at the ranch. In some situations where they live, there is little vegetation and the absence of seed-producing plants must be a limiting factor in the abundance of these mice.

Of all the peromyscines in the park, canyon mice are the most brightly colored.

CACTUS MOUSE
Peromyscus eremicus

Description. A medium-sized peromyscine with a tail that is sufficiently sparsely haired that annulations are evident and *without* a prominent terminal tuft of hairs. Ears of medium size and without edging of white. Skull can be distinguished by absence of accessory lophs on upper molars (usually absent in canyon mouse also); the premaxillae extend behind the nasals (do *not* in canyon mouse). Overall length, 7½ to 8½ inches (187 to 215 mm); tail, 3¾ to 4½ inches (92 to 115 mm); hind foot, about ⅞ inch (21 mm); ear, about ⅞ inch (21 mm).

Distribution. See map, p. 134.

Habits. Cactus mice are the principal white-footed mouse inhabitants of the inner parts of the canyon, except for the rocky walls where canyon mice live. Cactus mice inhabit the blackbrush–greasebush–prickly pear association of the Tonto Plateau. The only place that they occur on the North Rim is within the Inner Gorge along the Colorado River, as near the mouths of some of the North Rim creeks, although one specimen is labeled as "Bright Angel Point." Cactus mice do not get onto the top of Shiva Temple, although they might inhabit some other buttes that are less high and have flora similar to that of the Tonto Plateau. Although common within the canyon, these mice are found on the top of the South Rim only near

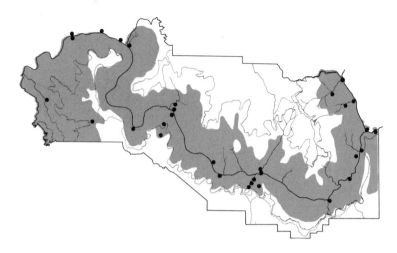

the top of Topocoba Canyon at Hilltop and near Bass Camp. Cactus mice fill the niche of the deer mice in the arid parts of the canyon.

Cactus mice live in a variety of places — crevices in the rocks, burrows abandoned by other animals, piles of debris, and clumps of cacti and yucca. They eat nearly anything that is available, even man's food supply. When Vernon Bailey and C. Hart Merriam were studying mammals within the canyon, Merriam wrote, "I was forced to place my scanty stock of provisions in a small tree for protection; but even there it was not safe, for the mice are excellent climbers, and I shot one by moonlight as it peered down at me from a low branch." He found cactus mice there to be "excessively abundant, outnumbering all the other mammals collectively."[27] Like other peromyscines, cactus mice are completely nocturnal.

DESERT WOOD RAT
Neotoma lepida

Description. One of the smaller wood rats with a tail that is not bushy. Fur on the back yellowish brown to grayish brown; fur on underparts whitish or buffy. All wood rats in the park have tails that are about three-fourths the length of the head and body and are

---

[27] C. Hart Merriam, "Results of a Biological Survey of the San Francisco Mountain Region and Desert of the Little Colorado, Arizona," *North American Fauna*, 3 (1890): 62.

about the size of the barn rat. The species of wood rats in the park differ in bushiness of the tail, coloration of the fur at its base and in the throat region, and general size, including length of the hind foot. There are important differences in skull and teeth. Overall length, 10¾ to 12 inches (275 to 305 mm); tail, 4¼ to 5¼ inches (108 to 132 mm); hind foot, 1¼ inches (31 mm).

Distribution.

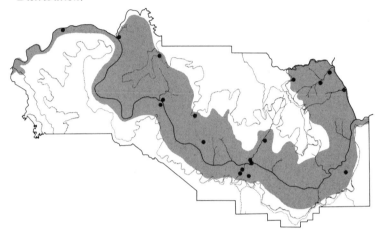

Habits. Desert wood rats on the North Rim live among the rocks and the bases of cliffs. On the South Rim much of this habitat is occupied by Stephen's wood rat, so desert wood rats inhabit the blackbrush–prickly pear–greasebush association of the Tonto Plateau. Cactus and agave or mescal provide excellent cover and protection from enemies as well as a source of food.

On the North Rim desert wood rats are found in the piñon-juniper and sagebrush areas near Point Sublime, but back under rocks which overhang the dry creek beds. Along the rocky rim they are in close association with bushy-tailed wood rats, but desert wood rats live under rocks where it is roomy and bushy-tails live in the deep fissures of the rocks. In both places desert wood rats feed extensively on piñon nuts for they had carried the cones to their houses and there scaled them. At the bottom of the North Rim those rats near the mouth of Bright Angel Creek live at the bases of the cliffs and among the rocks and cactus. A few houses were built under mesquite. The habitat here is much the same as on the Tonto Plateau across the river.

Five species of wood rats are found within the park. Three live only south of the river, one only north, and the desert wood rat lives on both sides. At several places on the South Rim three species live together, for example, at Indian Garden: desert, white-throated, and Mexican; and at Grand Canyon Village: Stephen's, white-throated, and Mexican.

Desert wood rats, like all wood rats, build conspicuous, conical houses. Theirs are usually built around the bases of shrubs, cacti, or in crevices in rocks. Materials, carried to the house, consist of sticks, cut stems and branches, leaves, and any intriguing objects including tin cans, bottle caps, droppings of larger mammals, and stones. The nest, made of finer material, often the shredded bark of the piñon or juniper, is placed well down inside the house. Some studies have shown that only about one out of every three houses is occupied. The others are temporary retreats. Desert wood rats feed on piñon nuts, mesquite beans, bark of numerous shrubs and plants, including cacti, and various seeds.

STEPHEN'S WOOD RAT
Neotoma stephensi

Description. About the same size as the desert wood rat except that tail is exceedingly hairy or semibushy and the dusky color extends down the top of the foot a third of the way below the ankle. Overall length, 10¾ to 12¾ inches (275 to 325 mm); tail, 4¾ to 5¾ inches (120 to 145 mm); hind foot, about 1¼ inches (32 mm).

Distribution. See map, p. 137.

Habits. Stephen's wood rats live in rocky places at the edge of the piñon-juniper association of the South Rim. They may move into man-made rock walls, for we found them in such a situation near the school athletic field of the Village. Since their houses may be far back in a rubble of rocks, large stick nests are not so obvious as with some other species. Stephen's wood rat is often closely associated with the white-throated wood rat on the South Rim. At Cedar Mountain

136

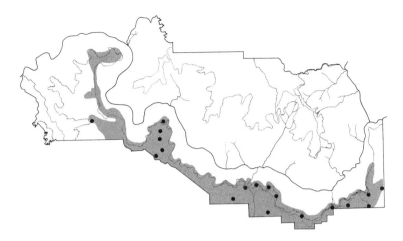

Stephen's were more in the piñon-juniper, white-throats more in the sagebrush-yucca-cholla, but the two species definitely overlapped. At Pasture Wash Stephen's were caught in the higher, more deeply undercut rocks, white-throats in the smaller rocks.

Stephen's wood rats feed on a variety of seeds, leaves, and barks. We also found instances of their eating ephedra.

WHITE-THROATED WOOD RAT
Neotoma albigula

Description. A large wood rat with a large, long tail that is haired but not bushy. Hairs on the throat white all the way to their bases. Hind feet of medium length but the sole not furred. Overall length, 12½ to 13¾ inches (315 to 350 mm); tail, 5½ to 6½ inches (140 to 165 mm); hind foot, about 1⅜ inches (33.5 mm).

Distribution. See map, p. 139.

Habits. White-throated wood rats live in the blackbrush–greasebush–prickly pear association of the Tonto Platform and in the drier, more deserty parts of the top of the South Rim, as at Hilltop, Pasture Wash, and Cedar Mountain. But sometimes they live in the piñons and junipers or in fractures in the canyon wall.

All wood rats are good house-builders, but white-throated wood rats are among the best. They cut branches, cactus pads, and leaves to

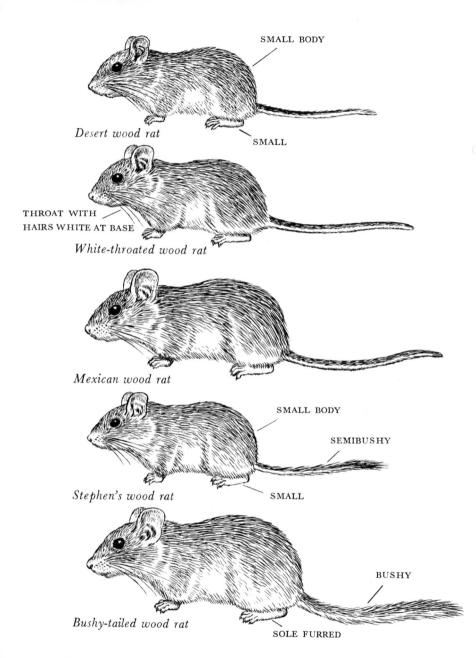

SMALL BODY

Desert wood rat

SMALL

THROAT WITH
HAIRS WHITE AT BASE

White-throated wood rat

Mexican wood rat

SMALL BODY

SEMIBUSHY

Stephen's wood rat

SMALL

BUSHY

Bushy-tailed wood rat

SOLE FURRED

Five species of wood rats in the park. (When comparing features, note the relative size of the body and the length of the tail.)

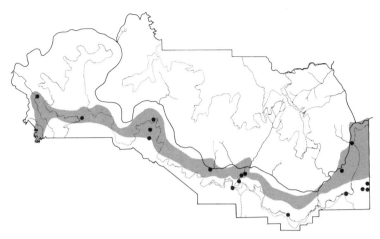

incorporate in their houses. Then they pick up anything loose to add to the structure — bottles, cans, mule droppings, bones, papers, or even mouse-traps. Houses may be as much as 4 feet high with numerous entrances opening to a maze of tunnels which end up at the inner nest. Food items are usually stored somewhere in the house. Wood from the houses of wood rats has provided kindling for campfires of many persons within the canyon.

Food of white-throats consists of cactus fruits, cactus pads, juniper berries, leaves from bushes, and the bark from stems. Leaves that are stored in the house are much like well-cured hay, for they are nearly as green as if they were just cut. All wood rats are excellent climbers and debark the limbs of bushes of all sizes. Droppings are in the form of black, half-inch-long pellets, always readily conspicuous. Some females we caught in mid-July were nursing young, so one would suspect that these were born in late June. Whether they have more than one litter each year is not known.

MEXICAN WOOD RAT
Neotoma mexicana

Description. Mexican wood rats are only slightly larger than white-throats but differ in having the hairs on the throat grayish at their bases rather than all white. Underparts often grayish with a brown spot on the chest between the forelegs. Overall length, 13 to 15 inches (330 to 380 mm); tail, 5⅛ to 7 inches (130 to 175 mm); hind foot, about 1½ inches (36.5 mm).

Distribution. South Rim only. See map under bushy-tailed wood rat.

Habits. Mexican wood rats are rock-dwellers of the higher parts of the South Rim. They prefer the ponderosa pine forest but where there are outcroppings of rocks. Frequently they are along the edge of the rim, or just below it, and sometimes in the piñon-juniper belt where there are rocks. They will not hesitate to live in or under a building and are excellent climbers. Often these wood rats occupy much the same habitat as the rock squirrel.

Mexican wood rats will build elaborate houses, but they may allow some other structure to serve as a house and then build very little. The wood rat that was seen by a group of visitors as it was being swallowed by a gopher snake at Yavapai Point probably was a Mexican wood rat. They have numerous enemies. Females may have two litters per year. One caught on June 22 was nursing young and also was pregnant. Other females were pregnant in mid-August. They eat a variety of shrubs and forbs as well as pine needles. Many specimens collected by us in the summer were infected with warbles, the larval stage of a flylike insect that develops beneath the skin of the rat. A common place for such warbles is on the throat and under the base of the tail. One Mexican wood rat had three warbles, each nearly an inch long. These must bother the rats and make them more susceptible to predators.

BUSHY-TAILED WOOD RAT
Neotoma cinerea

Description. Bushy-tailed wood rats can be distinguished from all other species within the park by their very bushy tails, large bodies, and large hind feet. The fur is long and a special dermal gland on the abdomen produces a distinctive odor. Overall length, 13¼ to 16⅞ inches (335 to 425 mm); tail, 5½ to 7½ inches (140 to 190 mm); hind foot, about 1⅝ inches (41 mm).

Distribution. North Rim only.

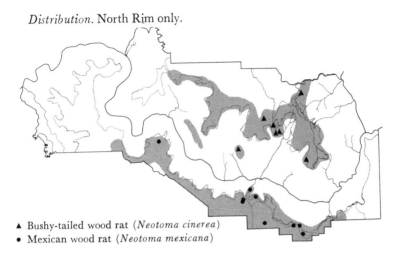

▲ Bushy-tailed wood rat (*Neotoma cinerea*)
● Mexican wood rat (*Neotoma mexicana*)

Habits. Bushy-tailed wood rats are inhabitants of the rocky rim on the north side of the canyon. They build their houses in crevices in the rocks, and the north cliffs provide an ideal situation, fairly free of predators. Bushy-tails get sufficiently far down the slopes that they have successfully bridged the divide and populated Shiva Temple. Houses of bushy-tails may not appear too large for they are usually well concealed, but they consist of a variety of objects, sometimes many bushelfuls, such as sticks, rocks, bone, bark, and any of man's objects, such as cans, cloth, or bottles, if they are available. Where bushy-tailed wood rats live in the canyon, they do not frequently come into contact with man and therefore have little opportunity to pack off his objects or to trade a stick or stone for a spoon, a piece of soap, or even a watch. However, some do live back from the rimrock and some took to living in the attic of the old ranger station, in the mule barns, and around some other structures.

Bushy-tails often have specific areas where they urinate and others where they defecate. Over many generations, accumulations of these waste products are noticeable. Young are born sometime in late June or early July; females taken in mid-July were nursing young. In early August young were out of the nest and foraging for themselves, judging from our trapping, but they were less than one-third grown. Bushy-tails store large quantities of food, especially foliage, in rock crevices. In late summer the store piles are increased for winter use.

After Harold Anthony visited Shiva Temple, he reported that "two distinct varieties of wood rats or pack rats lived among the rocks and, less frequently, among the trees."[28] Of the specimens he collected and I have examined from Shiva, all are bushy-tails. If any other kind was there, it might be the desert wood rat, the only other species found on the North Rim.

Long-tailed vole

Mexican vole

LONG-TAILED VOLE
Microtus longicaudus

Description. A species of vole or meadow mouse of brownish color heavily intermixed with black, underparts grayish. Ears short and nearly lost in the fur. All voles have short tails, but this is one of the longer-tailed species, with the tail about one-half the length of the head and body or one-third of the total length. Females have two pairs of pectoral mammae and two pairs of inguinal mammae. Overall length, 6½ to 7½ inches (168 to 188 mm); tail, 2 to 2½ inches (49 to 63 mm); hind foot, about ⅞ inch (21 mm).

[28] Harold E. Anthony, "The Facts about Shiva," *Natural History*, 40 (1937): 775.

Distribution. North Rim only. See map, p. 144.

Habits. Long-tailed voles or meadow mice are inhabitants of the meadows and grassy valleys of the North Rim. In many of these places the grass is exceedingly tall and in nearly all cases the area is moist — from either a spring or a lake. Voles make runways through the grass and these serve as trails to food, avenues of escape, or feeding areas. Such runways lead eventually to the entrances to underground burrows where the voles nest and hide. Runways may be used as much during the day as night. Fresh grass cuttings or fresh feces are an indication that voles are currently using the runways. Actually, long-tailed voles make less well-defined runways than do some other species.

During the winter when snow is deep, voles burrow through the snow to the branches of bushes to feed on the bark. However, their principal food is grass. Long-tailed voles do not hesitate to take to water and have been known to swim and dive readily. Sometimes these voles live some distance from water, as at Point Imperial, and in other areas they are known to live in less moist places than they usually do on the North Rim.

In Nevada long-tailed voles produce young from May through October, with the litter size usually five or six. The production of young may be much the same in the park. These voles are preyed upon by a wide variety of carnivores including owls, hawks, and snakes.

MEXICAN VOLE
Microtus mexicanus

Description. A small vole with an exceptionally short tail which is only a little more than one-fourth the length of head and body or about one-fifth the total length. Coloration about the same as the long-tailed vole but the underparts often tipped with brown. Length of hind feet more than half the length of the tail. Females with only one pair of pectoral mammae and one pair of inguinal mammae. Overall length, 4¼ to 5⅜ inches (110 to 136 mm); tail, 1 to 1⅜ inches (25 to 35 mm); hind foot, about ¾ inch (18 mm).

Distribution. South Rim only. See map, p. 144.

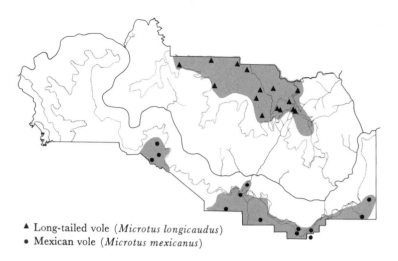

▲ Long-tailed vole (*Microtus longicaudus*)
● Mexican vole (*Microtus mexicanus*)

Habits. Mexican voles are inhabitants of grassy places on the South Rim. The grassy situations are much drier than those where long-tailed voles live. The grass may also be quite sparse. Runways in the grass lead to holes of underground burrows. Some places, as at Grapevine Tank and in Long Jim Canyon, old abandoned tunnels of pocket gophers serve as the underground burrows of Mexican voles. Small patches of grass, as are found at Indian Garden, provide sufficient food and protection for small colonies. Where conditions are satisfactory, Mexican voles live in colonies or at least are concentrated. We even found them living in sagebrush at Pasture Wash and Cedar Mountain and in man-made rock walls at Grand Canyon Village in association with Merriam's shrews, Stephen's wood rats, and rock squirrels.

In early August nearly all females taken were pregnant and some were nursing young that were fully furred but the eyes unopened. Probably all mature females have at least two litters per year. Undoubtedly many carnivores must prey upon these voles, for otherwise their numbers would soon get out of check. Mexican voles are as active during the day as the night, and often can be seen scooting along runways.

OLD WORLD MICE AND RATS (Family Muridae)

The house mouse, Norway rat, and black rat are members of this family, all of which have been introduced into North America. The house mouse is the only member of the family found to date within Grand Canyon.

HOUSE MOUSE
Mus musculus

Description. This well-known, nonnative mouse is characterized by its brownish-gray color above and below, scaly and thinly haired tail with the color on the underside not much lighter than that on top, and upper incisor teeth with a notch at the tip when viewed from the side. Females with five pairs of mammary glands. Overall length, about 6¾ inches ($\pm$ 165 mm); tail, about 3 inches ($\pm$ 75 mm); hind foot, about 1¾ inches (18 mm).

Distribution. Known only from Grand Canyon Village.

Habits. House mice are not native to North America but were introduced when boats and supplies arrived from overseas. These mice are closely associated with man, especially his buildings and food, and in many places do not live the year around in the out-of-doors. Often during the warmer months and when feed is available in the fields, house mice live in the wild, but as adverse conditions arise they move into man's shelters — barns, houses, and other structures.

The first known capture of a house mouse in Grand Canyon was in the Village at the home of naturalist E. D. McKee on July 25, 1935. Subsequently, specimens were taken at the mule barns and at Babbitt's store. Once house mice become established, they usually persist and spread in spite of efforts to eradicate them.

Norway rats (*Rattus norvegicus*) are not known in the wild in Grand Canyon, but one specimen was caught in the Harvey warehouse on November 3, 1958. This was a piebald inividual — black and white in color — not unlike some rats used in laboratory work but unlike feral rats. Probably this was an escaped pet; additional Norway rats have not been seen or caught in the park.

PORCUPINES (Family Erethizontidae)

Porcupines are large, seemingly sluggish rodents nearly the size of beavers, covered with both long spines and hair.

PORCUPINE
Erethizon dorsatum

Description. Sharp spines, often called quills, cover all except the underparts which have black hair; these black hairs, tipped with yellow, are dispersed among the spines. Tail short. Nails dark, often black. In winter, pelage is denser and longer. Ears relatively small and hardly visible. Overall length, 26 to 33 inches (660 to 840 mm); tail, 7 to 9 inches (175 to 235 mm); hind foot, about 4 inches (100 mm).

Distribution. See map, p. 147.

Habits. Porcupines are readily recognized, for no other mammal in North America is so well protected by an armor of long spines. "Porkies" use this protective covering only in defense. They are unable to throw their spines or quills. Since the spines are modified hairs and since hair is constantly being shed, some of the spines are shed and fall out when a porcupine shakes its body or tail. The numerous barbs on each spine make them difficult to remove once they have been driven into flesh.

On the North Rim porcupines are inhabitants of the forests. When

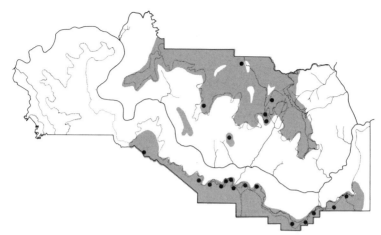

not in trees, we found that they took refuge in large holes back under large rocks. Judging from the amount of quills near some of these holes, porcupines have been inhabiting them for several generations. On the South Rim porcupines live in the ponderosa pine and piñon-juniper forests but also at distances away from forests. For example, along Pasture Wash we caught a "porky" on the dam of a dry tank. The animal had dug a large hole that very much resembled the hole of a badger. This animal had been feeding on herbaceous plants similar to those that grew on the dam and not like those elsewhere in the vicinity.

The usual food of the porcupine is the cambium layer, immediately under the bark, of various pines. They readily climb trees to reach a suitable part of the trunk where they methodically debark it to reach the sap-filled cambium. They also feed on grasses, seeds, and other herbaceous plants. One observed along the Cape Royal Road was feeding on the heads of plants growing on the shoulder of the road, sitting on its haunches and using its forefeet to bring the plants to its mouth. They probably feed more on conifers during the winter and more on leafy vegetation during the summer.

Mating may take place as late as early August, for naturalist Charles Bogert found that nearly all adults were traveling in pairs at that time.[29] A young porcupine, sufficiently young that there was

[29] *Grand Canyon Nature Notes*, 8, no. 1 (1933): 137.

much black hair but few quills, was reportedly seen June 27 on Buggelin Hill and another baby was captured at a checking station in August. Therefore, it is not clear when young are born. On the Kaibab Plateau two females gave birth to young shortly before May 9; three others were pregnant on this date. In each case there was but a single young.

Porcupines are primarily nocturnal and crepuscular (active in twilight) and thus are not readily seen unless ensconced in a tree. However, they are quite common on both rims. Ranger Bent counted eight between Grand Canyon Village and the old Grand Canyon airport. Coyotes and bobcats may try to feed on porcupines. Naturalist McKee saw a "porky" and a coyote together in the lights of his car. They apparently had been fighting. On the North Rim some are killed and eaten by mountain lions. In many areas automobiles are the greatest killer of porcupines.

EVEN-TOED HOOFED MAMMALS (Artiodactyla)

Artiodactyla or even-toed ungulates include pigs, deer, pronghorn, sheep, cattle, and relatives. They usually have two toes, sometimes four, and the toes have terminal hooves. Some have a complex, four-chambered stomach which permits them to chew a cud (ruminate).

DEER, ELK, AND MOOSE (Family Cervidae)

Antlers are present in male cervids (and in female caribou and reindeer). These are shed and replaced annually. When the antlers are being formed, they are covered with skin or "velvet." When fully formed, the velvet is rubbed off, exposing the hard, bony core.

Elk are not now, nor ever have been, resident within the park. Some may filter in on rare occasions from the national forest just south of the South Rim, but they are transients.

MULE DEER
Odocoileus hemionus

Description. A large deer with large ears, especially conspicuous in antlerless animals. Tail white or tan but conspicuously tipped with black. Males have antlers that are dichotomously branched. Overall (total) length from nose to tip of tail: males, about 6 feet ($\pm$ 1,850 mm), females, about 5½ feet ($\pm$ 1,630 mm); tail, about 7 inches ($\pm$ 180 mm); hind foot from heel to tip of hoof: males, about 1¾ feet ($\pm$ 530 mm), females, about 1½ feet ($\pm$ 470 mm). Bucks of the North Rim usually weigh between 160 and 190 pounds, some as much as 270 pounds.

Distribution. North and South rims and, in limited numbers, within the canyon.

Habits. Mule deer are present on both rims as well as on the plateaus, some of the buttes, and down within the canyon. In the summertime they are especially numerous on the North Rim. Some deer at the Village on the South Rim have become pets and are especially conspicuous.

Fawns are born on the North Rim between June 12 and July 10, on the South Rim between June 1 and July 7, although some fawns have been dropped as early as March 14. Frequently twins are born. Females prefer the yellow pine forests when the fawns are born. The gestation period is approximately seven months, although it is variable. Breeding (rutting) occurs between mid-November and mid-December on the North Rim and continues until mid-January or late January on the South Rim. Necks of the bucks swell noticeably during the rut and battles between males are frequent. These battles are to decide supremacy among males, and sometimes they result in severe if not fatal injuries. A pair of four-point bucks had locked their antlers during such a fight. One had a broken neck and the other was liberated only after the rangers had sawed the antlers.

Antlers are shed in late February and March; new antlers appear in mid-April. Antlers are nearly full grown in early August but the tips are still soft. The covering over the growing antlers, called velvet, is rubbed off when the antlers have reached maximum size for the year. Such shedding usually takes place in September and much rubbing of antlers occurs then. The number of points on the antlers is not indicative of the age of bucks, for old bucks have fewer points but heavier main beams than do prime, although younger, bucks. Variation is shown in the number of points in three deer on the South Rim known to be one year old; one had antlers with one spike, one with three points, and one with three points plus an eye-guard.[30]

Mule deer are especially numerous on the Kaibab Plateau north of the canyon. Many of these move onto the North Rim. Because of the severity of the winters on the North Rim, deer must move either north or south to the very edge of the rim where the warmer canyon air provides suitable areas for yarding or congregating. These are located at such places as Point Sublime, Cape Royal, Cape Final, and Cape York. At some of these places overbrowsing occurs. The deer also may move down within the canyon, for they are sure-footed and move along the ledges nearly as well as bighorn. They are present along some of the creeks and on Shiva Temple. At Bright Angel Point, where deer are common in the summer, the first one did not appear until April 27 in 1928, there were eighteen two days later,

[30] *Ibid.*, 3, no. 5 (1928): 3.

and by May there were forty.[31] When winter storms unload excessive snow on the South Rim, more deer are present at Indian Garden, so some deer on the South Rim may temporarily move below the rim.

Deer were never as numerous on the South as on the North Rim. Therefore, several transplants have been made from north to south, one as early as 1927. Five years earlier an attempt was made to drive deer from the north through the Inner Gorge to the south side, but this failed. In 1927 ten fawns were transported via Lee's Ferry to the South Rim; eight survived at least until fall.[32] In September, 1929, eight fawns were flown to the South Rim from the North. Prior to these transplants, park rangers on the South Rim said deer tracks were seldom found. By 1945 a browse-line, indicative of overabundance, was beginning to appear on the South Rim, and some deer were trapped and moved elsewhere.

Mule deer are browsers, nibbling on leaves and buds of trees, bushes, and grasses. One analysis of thirty-four stomachs indicated these food items: 39 per cent juniper, 19 per cent cliff rose, 6 per cent piñon, 14 per cent sagebrush, and the rest a variety of things. In another analysis of stomachs of sixteen deer taken entirely on the North Rim, the results were: 19 per cent aspen, 14 per cent ponderosa pine, 8 per cent mushrooms, 18 per cent "weeds," 6 per cent Gambel oak, and the remainder, various items. They may browse on cactus, Mormon tea, rabbitbrush, and wild carrot, but the favorite miscellaneous items are bitterbrush, apache plume, wild rose, red currant, shadscale, and silk-tassel brush. The poisonous amanitas mushrooms are eaten by the park deer with no ill effects. Deer that develop the habit of feeding on "handouts" around campgrounds and villages, as well as on garbage, continue this in preference to normal food and often grow exceedingly thin on such fare.

Probably coyotes are the main predators of deer within the canyon, and they are successful in taking fawns, young, and sick deer. On the North Rim the few mountain lion that occur within the park feed on deer. Nose flies, tapeworms, and pinkeye are known to affect and weaken some deer in the park.

[31] *Ibid.*, 2, no. 12 (1928): 2.
[32] *Ibid.*, 2, no. 5 (1927): 1.

Mule deer undergo a molt during late August and September when the worn, reddish or tan coat of summer is replaced by one that is more gray or bluish gray. Another molt occurs in the spring, usually in May, when the more reddish coat of summer is acquired. Fawns lose their spots by September.

PRONGHORN (Family Antilocapridae)

Pronghorns or pronghorned antelope have unique horns with bony cores over which there is a horn or horny sheath; the horn is forked and is shed and replaced annually. No other artiodactyl has a horn core with a horn that is shed annually. The horn consists of fused hair. Both males and females possess horns but they are smaller in females.

PRONGHORN or PRONGHORNED ANTELOPE
Antilocapra americana

Description. As described for the family, this is the only artiodactyl with forked or branched horns that are shed and replaced annually. There are conspicuous white areas on the sides and rump, and two white bands across the throat; upper parts are tan; white hair on the rump is long and can be erected. Males have an overall length of about 4½ feet (± 1,370 mm); tail, about 6 inches (140 mm); hind foot, about 16 inches (420 mm); females are about 10 per cent smaller. Weight of males is usually between 75 and 125 pounds.

Distribution. Formerly on South Rim only, including the Tonto Plateau. May still enter the park from the south.

Habits. Pronghorns are fleet-footed animals of the open, mostly flat land. At one time they were abundant in the piñon flats between San Francisco Peaks and the South Rim and over the Kanab Plateau between the Vermillion Cliffs and the Colorado River. Pronghorns have never been especially numerous within the park because of the nature of the terrain and the absence of much free water on the South Rim. Places where they might do well on the South Rim are the Great Thumb, Pasture Wash, and between Desert View and Cedar Mountain. Sources of water would need to be provided. Pronghorns have always been numerous in the Tusayan forest just south of the park.

The Tonto Plateau, a fairly flat area below the South Rim at about 3,000 feet elevation, was thought to be a good place to transplant pronghorns. Therefore, in 1924 twelve young animals, six males and six females, were brought from Reno, Nevada, and transported to the plateau on muleback. Eleven reached the area safely and later moved to the vicinity of Indian Garden. Since the original eleven pronghorn were semitame, they presented certain problems. One buck attacked the trail caretaker several times, one doe became a camp nuisance, and another buck developed fighting tendencies with other members of the herd. Some of the animals suffered from the heat and supplemental feeding was necessary. Nevertheless, the pronghorns eventually adjusted to the conditions and the available forage and persist around Indian Garden. In 1934 the herd was believed to number twenty-one or more, perhaps over thirty in 1944.

Some reports of pronghorn on the South Rim, with the year of reporting, are: ½ mile south of Village (1932); three at Buggelin Hill (1934); twenty near Plateau Point (1935); five ¼ mile south of Shoshone Point (1939); two near Hopi Watchtower (1938); Pasture Wash (1938); west of Twin Tanks (1940); near Desert View (1949); Coronado Point (1954); four near Bucklar Ranch (1957);

two at Buggelin Hill (1958); nineteen near Hilltop (1959); south entrance to park (1959).

At Indian Garden pronghorns feed on catclaw, blackbrush, wild grape, cottonwood, grasses, and the succulent stalks of the yucca. At Pasture Wash they were seen feeding on saltbush and bunch grass. Pronghorns feed on grasses and forbs in the spring and summer and turn more to browse in the fall and winter. Young pronghorns or kids are probably preyed upon by bobcats and coyotes.

SHEEP, BISON, GOATS, AND CATTLE (Family Bovidae)

Bovids have horns which are formed over and supported by bony cores. Horns are not shed but usually are added to continuously. Horns are often present in both males and females.

BIGHORN or MOUNTAIN SHEEP
Ovis canadensis

Description. Bighorns are the native sheep of North America; males have large curled horns, females have smaller, nearly straight horns. Large, yellowish-white rump patch. Tail small and not conspicuous. Color of upper parts light brown or tan. In males, overall length, about 5¾ feet (± 1,750 mm); tail, about 4 inches

($\pm$ 100 mm); hind foot, about 18 inches ($\pm$ 450 mm). Females are about 10 per cent smaller.

Distribution. Mostly within the canyon on both sides of the Colorado River. Probably more numerous west of Kaibab trails.

Habits. Bighorns or mountain sheep are inhabitants of the crags, cliffs, and precipices of the canyon. The inaccessibility of many parts of the canyon is their forte, far removed from predators and man. Only rarely do bighorns wander onto the tops of the rims, and then their presence is so unusual that records are made of it. For example, one ewe was noted at the top of Bright Angel Trail on two consecutive days in May, 1927, and then she disappeared. In March, 1928, another bighorn, or perhaps the same one, fell in ahead of a returning mule train, 700 feet from the top of Bright Angel Trail, and lead it to the top, and then disappeared. A ram was seen near the viewing area at Havasupai Point in November, 1933, and apparently remained in that vicinity for several days. Another ram watched in December, 1927, as men worked on the Yavapai Point observation station. Occasionally, they are seen just below the rim in front of El Tovar Hotel. One has the impression that in areas where they are not hunted, bighorns become less timid and more curious. Hikers on trails are most likely to see bighorns near Indian Garden, on Cedar Ridge, and below Yaki and Yavapai points.

Records of observations of bighorns kept by the Park Service indicate that they have been seen in most of the side canyons and most of the creeks cutting the Tonto Plateau on the south side of the park and as far west as the mouth of Havasu Creek. Vernon Bailey saw numbers of them on the side of Battleship Butte. Reports from the north side are fewer: various places along Bright Angel Canyon, Cliff Springs, and near Kanab Creek. Bighorns normally remain above the Inner Gorge of the river and below the rim. However, they are frequently seen by river boats as they water at the river's edge. Some early estimates of mountain sheep in Grand Canyon area are: 1924, 100 bighorns; 1925, 500; 1926, 590; 1927, 590; 1929, 500. In 1969 the estimate was 150. Indians indicate that in former times there were many more bighorns in the canyon, but there was a big die-off. This may have resulted from diseases they con-

155

tracted from domestic sheep that were grazed beyond the park boundaries. Also bighorns were heavily hunted during the early mining days in what is now the park.

Ewes probably drop their lambs in March, but little is known of this in the canyon and it may be as early as February or as late as April. Lambs about one-third grown have been reported in November. The mating or rutting season extends from August to October. Adults have a fall and a spring molt. One would suspect that the bighorns in the canyon feed on the fruits of prickly pear, yucca, various grasses, agave, and burro brush.

HORSES AND RELATIVES
(Perissodactyla, Family Equidae)

Horses are odd-toed (one), hoofed mammals with the third digit being the only functional toe in each foot. Horses and donkeys do not natively live within Grand Canyon, but burros or donkeys have been released therein, have multiplied, live totally in the wild, and now are part of the fauna.

BURRO
Equus asinus

In 1919, when the canyon became a national park, wild burros were abundant on the Tonto Plateau, perhaps numbering as many as 3,000. Prospectors had released and abandoned these animals, and they multiplied and thrived on the Tonto. Burro brush and grasses were overgrazed and the animals with their sharp hooves dug out the prickly pear cactus and agave and ate the roots.

The large number of burros was reduced by the Park Service in the early 1920's, but the remainder continued to multiply and it is still necessary to remove periodically as many as possible of these burros from the park. Nearly 3,000 have been removed since the twenties. It is desirable to remove these burros since they compete with the bighorn and mule deer for food and water. After the original extensive reduction campaigns, wild flowers appeared on the Tonto that had not been seen for many years.[33] Reportedly the continued inbreeding of the population within the park produced a small burro of an average height for adults of 4 feet.

At the present time wild burros are most abundant as follows: South Rim on the Tonto Plateau from Red Canyon to Forster Canyon; on the North Rim in Shinumo Creek drainage.

[33] P. P. Patraw, *Grand Canyon Nature Notes,* 4, no. 7 (1930): 44.

GAZETTEER OF LOCALITIES

Mammals have been collected at numerous places within the park. These localities are given in the section "Specimens of Mammals Taken in Grand Canyon" and many of the localities are mentioned in the various accounts. For convenience, a gazetteer of these localities is given. Localities on the North Rim and those within the canyon but *north* of the Colorado River are listed below. Numbers in the list correspond to numbered spots north of the river on the map (p. 159). The numbers start at 1 again for those localities *south* of the river, and these are given later under "South Side Localities."

NORTH SIDE LOCALITIES

1. "Powell Plateau"
2. Saddle Canyon
3. Powell Spring, 6,200 ft.
4. Muav Saddle; corral near Muav Trail
5. Swamp Point
6. Swamp Lake
7. 9 mi. E Swamp Point
8. Tipover Spring
9. 1 mi. NE Kanabownits Spring; Kanabownits Spring
10. 3 mi. S Kanabownits Spring
11. Point Sublime
12. Coffee Lake; Point Sublime Road near Coffee Lake
13. Shinumo Creek
14. Crystal Creek
15. Shiva Temple
16. Mouth Bright Angel Creek; Bright Angel Creek Campground between Phantom Ranch and Colorado River
17. Phantom Ranch
18. Bright Angel Canyon below Ribbon Falls

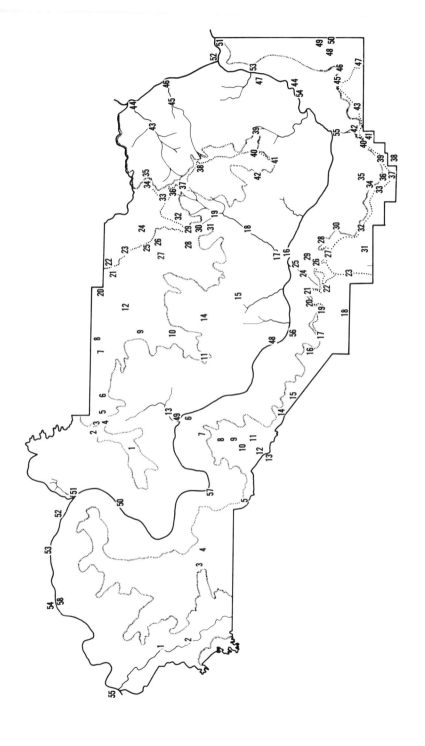

19. ½ mi. down Kaibab Trail; head Kaibab Trail; head Bright Angel Creek; Bright Angel Creek, Kaibab Plateau; Bright Angel Spring; CCC Camp overlooking Kaibab Trail
20. Fawn Springs
21. Road W-3 near north entrance
22. ½ mi. S North Rim entrance
23. Old Entrance Road
24. 5 mi. N Bright Angel Ranger Station; 5 mi. N, 1 mi. E Bright Angel Ranger Station
25. Robbers Roost; Robbers Roost Spring, 8,200 ft.; near mill site, Robbers Roost Ridge, 8,200 ft.
26. 5 mi. S North Rim Checking Station; Lindberg Hill Highway
27. The Basin
28. Marble Flats
29. Thompson Canyon, ½ mi. N Bright Angel Ranger Station
30. Harvey Camp, 8,300 ft.; North Rim Ranger Station; mule barn near headquarters; headquarters building; North Rim administration building; public campground; "near dormitory"
31. Bright Angel Point
32. Fuller Canyon, road E-2; Fuller Canyon, road W-2; Fuller Spring; Long Road in Thompson Canyon
33. Neal Spring; campground near Neal Spring; ½ mi. NE Neal Spring
34. 4 mi. NE Neal Spring
35. Point Imperial
36. Greenland Spring
37. Greenland Lake
38. Walhalla Plateau; Farview (first hairpin curve on Cape Royal Road, 1 mi. S Point Imperial–Neal Spring Junction); Snowshoe Cabin, 8,400 ft. (at Greenland Lake along Cape Royal Road)
39. Cape Final
40. 2 mi. N Cape Royal
41. Cape Royal
42. Point Honan
43. Nankoweap Canyon, 3 mi. from Colorado River, 3,600 ft.

44. Nankoweap Canyon and along Nankoweap Creek; Nankoweap Campground, Mile 53, 2,775 ft.
45. Kwagunt Creek, 2 mi. W and 3 mi. W Colorado River, 3,200 ft.
46. Kwagunt delta on Colorado River, 2,800 ft.
47. Chuar Creek
48. Mouth Crystal Creek, Mile 99
49. Hotauta Canyon, Mile 108, 2,266 ft.
50. Mile 128, 2,100 ft.
51. Mouth Tapeats Creek, Mile 134, 2,000 ft.
52. Deer Creek Falls, Mile 136, 1,925 ft., Kaibab National Forest
53. Mouth Fishtail Canyon, Mile 139, Kaibab National Forest
54. Mouth Kanab Creek, Mile 143.5, 1,900 ft., Kaibab National Forest
55. Mile 156 (upstream from mouth Havasu Creek), Grand Canyon National Monument

SOUTH SIDE LOCALITIES

1. Supai Canyon
2. Mouth Cataract Canyon
3. Hilltop
4. 1½ mi. E Hilltop
5. 7 mi. SE Hilltop
6. 6 mi. N Bass Camp
7. 1 mi. N Bass Camp
8. Bass Camp
9. Pasture Wash roads W-9 and W-9A
10. Pasture Wash
11. 3 mi. S Bass Camp, 6,400 ft.
12. ½ mi. N Pasture Wash Ranger Station; Pasture Wash Ranger Station; 1 mi. S Pasture Wash Ranger Station
13. 2 mi. S Pasture Wash Ranger Station
14. 4½ mi. SSE Pasture Wash Ranger Station
15. 6 mi. SSE Pasture Wash Ranger Station
16. Mesa Eremita
17. Hermits Rest; Hermit Trail above Hermit Basin; Hermit Basin
18. Rowes Well; ¾ mi. SW Rowes Well

19. Abyss; ¼ mi. S The Abyss
20. Mohave Point
21. Powell Memorial
22. Top of rim near Village; near Village at top of rim and just under rim; head Bright Angel Trail; Grand Canyon Village school; near El Tovar Hotel; Grand Canyon Village; visitor center; Village school athletic field
23. 3 mi. S Grand Canyon Village; south entrance station
24. Indian Garden; up trail from Indian Garden
25. 1½ mi. below Indian Garden; Tonto Plateau below Indian Garden; 1 mi. below Indian Garden; Garden Creek, 1½ mi. below Indian Garden; 1¾ mi. down trail from Indian Garden; 1¾ mi. below Indian Garden; 2 mi. down trail from Indian Garden; 2 mi. below Indian Garden; near bottom Bright Angel Trail
26. Yavapai Point; Yavapai Point Trail
27. Between Yavapai and Yaki points
28. Yaki Point; ¾ mi. E Yaki Point
29. Pipe Creek
30. Shoshone Point
31. Long Jim Canyon, 4 mi. E, 3 mi. S Grand Canyon Village
32. Grapevine Canyon
33. 2 mi. W, ½ mi. S Grandview Point
34. Grandview Point
35. Grandview Trail
36. 2 mi. W Grandview Point; 1 mi. W Grandview Point; Grandview; Hearst Ranch, Grandview
37. 1 mi. SE Grandview; Hearst Ranch Tank
38. Hull Tank; Hull Tank Ranger Station
39. 1 mi. W Buggelin Tank; 10 mi. E Grand Canyon (Village); Buggelin Hill; between Grandview and Moran points; Buggelin Tank, 10 mi. E, 5½ mi. S Grand Canyon Village
40. Moran Point
41. 1 mi. SW Moran Point
42. W side Zuni Point
43. Wayside Museum

44. Colorado River, foot Tanner Trail; McCormick Mine, foot Tanner Trail
45. Desert View; Desert View Checking Station; ¼ mi. SE Desert View
46. 1 mi. E, ½ mi. S Desert View Point; 1¼ mi. E Desert View Point; 1¾ mi. E Desert View Point
47. Route 64, SE park boundary; SE park boundary
48. W side Cedar Mountain, 6,500 ft.
49. N side Cedar Mountain, 6,500 ft.
50. E side Cedar Mountain, 6,500 ft.
51. On Little Colorado River, 1½ mi. E junction with Colorado River
52. At junction with Little Colorado River, Mile 61.5, 2,800 ft.
53. Palisades Creek, Mile 66, 2,675 ft.
54. Mile 70, 2,700 ft.
55. Hance Rapids, Mile 76.5, 2,600 ft.
56. Mouth Hermit Creek, Mile 95, 2,500 ft.
57. Elves Chasm, Mile 116.5, 2,100 ft.
58. S shore Colorado River, 100 yds. to ¼ mi. upstream from mouth Kanab Creek

SPECIMENS OF MAMMALS
TAKEN IN GRAND CANYON[1]

Sorex merriami leucogenys Osgood. NORTH RIM:[2] 5 mi. N, 1 mi. E Bright Angel Ranger Station, 1. SOUTH RIM: Grand Canyon Village school, 1; Long Jim Canyon, 4 mi. E, 3 mi. S Grand Canyon Village, 1; Buggelin Tank, 10 mi. E, 5½ mi. S Grand Canyon Village, 1.

Sorex nanus Merriam. NORTH RIM: 9 mi. E Swamp Point, 1 (GCM); Kaibab Lodge, VT Ranch (just outside park boundary), 1 (GCM).

Notiosorex crawfordi crawfordi (Coues). SOUTH RIM: Hermit Trail above Hermit Basin, 6,000 ft., 1 (GCM); near bottom Bright Angel Trail, 2,500 ft., 1 (GCM); Desert View Checking Station, 1 (GCM).

Myotis yumanensis yumanensis (H. Allen). NORTH RIM: mouth Bright Angel Creek, 10; Phantom Ranch, 1. SOUTH RIM: Supai Canyon, 11 (USBS); Hearst Ranch, Grandview, 1.

Myotis [lucifugus] occultus Hollister. None seen; reported from "South Rim."[3]

Myotis evotis evotis (H. Allen). NORTH RIM: CCC Camp overlooking Kaibab Trail, 2; ½ mi. S North Rim entrance, 2; Old

[1] Unless otherwise indicated, specimens are in the collection of the Museum of Natural History, University of Illinois. Abbreviations for some other museums are: GCM, Grand Canyon National Park Museum; USBS, U.S. Biological Surveys Collection; AM, American Museum; MNA, Museum of Northern Arizona; S. F. State, San Francisco State; BYU/MNA, jointly by Brigham Young University and Museum of Northern Arizona.

[2] NORTH RIM in this case means north of the Colorado River, but the locality may actually be within the canyon or up on the rim. Phantom Ranch and Cape Royal would both be listed as NORTH RIM. SOUTH RIM is everything south of the Colorado River.

[3] Bailey, "Mammals of the Grand Canyon Region."

Entrance Road, 1 (GCM); headquarters building, 1 (GCM); campground near Neal Spring, 4; Greenland Lake, 4. SOUTH RIM: locality not specified.[4]

Myotis thysanodes thysanodes Miller. NORTH RIM: campground near Neal Spring, 1. SOUTH RIM: Pasture Wash Ranger Station, 1; Hearst Ranch, Grandview, 21; Hull Tank Ranger Station, 2 (USBS); Buggelin Tank, 1; 1 mi. SW Moran Point, 1; Wayside Museum, 1 (GCM).

Myotis volans interior Miller. NORTH RIM: ½ mi. S North Rim entrance, 1; Greenland Lake, 1. SOUTH RIM: Pasture Wash, 1 (GCM); near El Tovar Hotel, 1 (GCM); Hearst Ranch, Grandview, 39.

Myotis californicus stephensi Dalquest. NORTH RIM: mouth Bright Angel Creek, 2,500 ft., 6; Phantom Ranch, 8 (2, UI; 1, GCM; 5, USBS); Bright Angel Point, 1 (GCM); Greenland Lake, 3; Hotauta Canyon, Mile 108, 2,266 ft., 1 (BYU/MNA). SOUTH RIM: Supai Canyon, 6 (USBS); Pasture Wash, 1; Grand Canyon Village, 2 (GCM); visitor center, 1 (GCM); Indian Garden, 4; Hearst Ranch, Grandview, 14; Government Hill, 1 (GCM); CCC Camp 819, 1 (GCM).

Myotis leibii melanorhinus (Merriam). SOUTH RIM: Hearst Ranch, Grandview, 4; near route 64, SE entrance, 1.

Lasionycteris noctivagans (Le Conte). SOUTH RIM: Grand Canyon Village, 1 (GCM).

Pipistrellus hesperus hesperus (H. Allen). NORTH RIM: Muav Saddle, 6,700 ft., 7; mouth Bright Angel Creek, 6; Greenland Lake, 7; Deer Creek Falls, Mile 136, Kaibab National Forest, 1,925 ft., 1 (BYU/MNA). SOUTH RIM: Supai Canyon, 2 (USBS); Pasture Wash Ranger Station, 5; Grand Canyon Village, 1 (GCM); Indian Garden, 1; 2½ mi. W, ½ mi. S Grandview, 1; Hearst Ranch, Grandview, 12; Hull Tank, 1; Buggelin Tank, 2; route 64 at SE entrance, 11; McCormick Mine, foot Tanner Trail, 2,000 ft., 1 (GCM); Cohinini Plateau, 7 (USBS).

Eptesicus fuscus pallidus Young. NORTH RIM: ½ mi. S entrance, 2; Greenland Lake, 3. SOUTH RIM: Harvey garage, Grand Canyon

---

[4] *Ibid.*, p. 40.

Village, 1 (GCM); Hearst Ranch, Grandview, 15; Hull Tank, 2 (1, USBS); route 64 at SE entrance, 4; Rain Tank, 2 (GCM); Old Williams Road, 1 (GCM).

Lasiurus borealis teliotis (H. Allen). NORTH RIM: Bright Angel Creek Campground between Phantom Ranch and Colorado River, 1.

Lasiurus cinereus cinereus (Palisot de Beauvois). NORTH RIM: Phantom Ranch, 1 (GCM).

Plecotus townsendii pallescens Miller. SOUTH RIM: Pasture Wash Ranger Station, 5; Hearst Ranch, Grandview, 13.

Antrozous pallidus pallidus (Le Conte). NORTH RIM: Phantom Ranch, 2 (GCM); Bright Angel Point, 1 (GCM); Cape Royal Road, 1 (GCM). SOUTH RIM: Pasture Wash, 1 (GCM); Grand Canyon Village, 4 (GCM); south entrance station (1958), 1 (GCM); Indian Garden, 1; Buggelin Tank, 1.

Tadarida brasiliensis mexicana (Saussure). NORTH RIM: Muav Saddle, 6,700 ft., 2. SOUTH RIM: Hance Rapids, Mile 76.5, 2,608 ft., 1 (BYU/MNA).

Ursus [Euarctos] americanus amblyceps Baird. No specimens. Sight records in text.

Ursus horribilis (subspecies?). No specimens.

Procyon lotor pallidus Merriam. Localities of reported occurrences are cited in the text.

Bassariscus astutus (subspecies either *arizonensis* Goldman or *nevadensis* Miller). NORTH RIM: mouth Bright Angel Creek, 1; Bright Angel Creek, Kaibab Plateau, 2 (USBS); North Rim Ranger Station, 1 (GCM). SOUTH RIM: Village, 1 (GCM). Additional records in text.

Mustela frenata arizonensis (Mearns). NORTH RIM: The Basin, 1; Bright Angel Point, 1 (GCM); VT Park (just outside park), 1 (USBS). SOUTH RIM: Village (Harvey mule barns), 1 (GCM). Additional record in text.

Lutra canadensis sonora Rhoads. Along Colorado River; no specimens. See text for records.

Spilogale putorius [gracilis] Merriam. NORTH RIM: Shiva Temple, 1 (S. F. State); mouth Bright Angel Creek, 2,500 ft., 4 (1, GCM). SOUTH RIM: Indian Garden, 1 (GCM); Bright Angel Trail, ½ mi.

below Indian Garden, 1; Bright Angel Trail, 1.1 mi. below Indian Garden, 1; bottom Grand Canyon, 2 (USBS).

Mephitis mephitis estor Merriam. SOUTH RIM: Hearst Ranch, 3; Hearst Ranch Tank, 1; Berry Ranch, 1 (GCM).

Taxidea taxus berlandieri Baird. SOUTH RIM: 3/4 mi. E Yaki Point, 1 (GCM). Other records in text.

Canis latrans mearnsi Merriam. NORTH RIM: Bright Angel Spring, 3 (USBS); 2 mi. S North Rim Checking Station, 1 (GCM). SOUTH RIM: Rowes Well, 2 (USBS); village, 1 (GCM); Berry Ranch, 1 (GCM); Hopi Point, 2 (USBS). Other records in text.

Canis lupus youngi Goldman. No specimens examined.

Urocyon cinereoargenteus scottii Mearns. NORTH RIM: Bright Angel Point, 1 (GCM). SOUTH RIM: Supai, 1 (USBS); "Grand Canyon," 1 (USBS); Indian Garden, 3,800 ft., 1 (USBS); Yaki Point, 1 (GCM); Desert View, 1 (GCM).

Felis concolor kaibabensis Nelson and Goldman. NORTH RIM: Powell Plateau, 8,700 ft., 1 (USBS); "Bright Angel," 1 (USBS).

Felis concolor azteca Merriam. See records in text.

Felis onca arizonensis Goldman. Reportedly from "about 4 mi. S canyon rim"; see text.

Lynx rufus baileyi Merriam. See records in text.

Sylvilagus audubonii warreni Nelson. SOUTH RIM: 1½ mi. E Hilltop, 1; 7 mi. SE Hilltop, 1; Pasture Wash Ranger Station, 3; Grand Canyon Village, 1; Long Jim Canyon, 1; 1 mi. SW Moran Point, 1; Desert View, 1 (GCM); 1¾ mi. E Desert View Point, 1; route 64, SE park boundary, 1; N side Cedar Mountain, 6,500 ft., 1; Trash Tank, 1 (USBS).

Sylvilagus nuttallii grangeri (J. A. Allen). NORTH RIM: Crystal Creek, 1 (GCM); Shiva Temple, 2 (AM).

Lepus californicus deserticola Mearns. NORTH RIM: Slide Tank, 1 (GCM). SOUTH RIM: 6 mi. SSE Pasture Wash Ranger Station, 1; Yaki Point, 1 (GCM).

[*Lepus townsendii townsendii* Bachman. Presence on North Rim hypothetical.]

Spermophilus [*Citellus*] *variegatus utah* (Merriam). NORTH RIM: Muav Saddle, 7,000 ft., 2; Swamp Point, 7,500 ft., 1; Shiva Temple, 2 (AM); Phantom Ranch, 6 (2, USBS; 4, GCM); Bright Angel

Point, 1 (GCM); 2 mi. N Cape Royal, 1 (GCM); Farview, 1 (GCM).

Spermophilus [Citellus] variegatus grammurus (Say). SOUTH RIM: Abyss, 1 (GCM); Grand Canyon (Village), 6,800 ft., 6 (1, USBS; 4, GCM; 1, UI); "Grand Canyon," 1 (Los Angeles County Museum); Indian Garden, 3,800 ft., 1 (USBS); Yavapai Point, 1 (GCM); Pipe Creek, 2 (USBS); 2 mi. W, ½ mi. S Grandview Point, 2; Hearst Ranch, Grandview, 1; between Grandview and Moran points, 1 (GCM); Desert View Point, 3; "Coconino Plateau," 4 (USBS).

Spermophilus [Citellus] spilosoma pratensis (Merriam). SOUTH RIM: 3 mi. S Bass Camp, 6,400 ft., 7 (USBS); Trash Tank (at park boundary), 1 (USBS).

Ammospermophilus [Citellus] leucurus cinnamomeus (Merriam). NORTH RIM: Nankoweap Canyon, 3 mi. from Colorado River, 3,600 ft., 4 (MNA); Kwagunt Creek, 2 mi. W Colorado River, 3,200 ft., 2 (MNA). SOUTH RIM: Indian Garden, 3,800 ft., 9 (5, USBS; 4, GCM); Pipe Creek, 2 (USBS); W side Cedar Mountain, 6,550 ft., 2; E side Cedar Mountain, 6,500 ft., 1.

Ammospermophilus [Citellus] leucurus tersus (Goldman). SOUTH RIM: 2 mi. S Pasture Wash Ranger Station, 1; 3 mi. S Pasture Wash Ranger Station, 1. Both records just south of park boundary but species known to occur within park.

Spermophilus [Callospermophilus] lateralis lateralis (Say). NORTH RIM: Swamp Lake, 7 (4, GCM); 1 mi. NE Kanabownits Spring, 1; Fawn Springs, 1; road W-3 near north entrance, 8; ½ mi. S North Rim entrance, 5; 5 mi. S North Rim Checking Station, 1 (GCM); Robbers Roost Spring, 8,700 ft., 1 (GCM); 5 mi. N, 1 mi. E Bright Angel Ranger Station, 1; The Basin, 3; North Rim administration building, 1; Bright Angel Point, 2; Thompson Canyon, ½ mi. N Bright Angel Ranger Station, 1; Fuller Canyon, road E-2, 3; Fuller Canyon, road W-2, 2; Neal Spring, 1; Point Imperial, 2; Greenland Spring, 2 (USBS); Bright Angel Ranger Station, 2. SOUTH RIM: Village school athletic field, 1.[5]

[5] See comments in Donald F. Hoffmeister, "Mammals New to Grand Canyon National Park, Arizona," *Plateau*, 28 (1955): 5.

Cynomys gunnisoni zuniensis Hollister. SOUTH RIM: Pasture Wash, 1 (GCM).

Eutamias dorsalis utahensis Merriam. NORTH RIM: Saddle Canyon, 1;[6] Muav Saddle, 7,000 ft., 1 (GCM); Point Sublime, 1 (GCM); Shiva Temple, 18 (AM); Kwagunt Creek, 2 mi. W Colorado River, 1 (MNA).

Eutamias dorsalis dorsalis (Baird). SOUTH RIM: Pasture Wash, junction of roads W-9A and W-9, 6,600 ft., 1; 4½ mi. SSE Pasture Wash Ranger Station, 1; Grand Canyon Village, 11 (8, GCM); Indian Garden, 3,800 ft., 2 (USBS); Shoshone Point, 1; Long Jim Canyon, 5; 2 mi. W, ½ mi. S Grandview Point, 2; Grandview, 7,150 ft., 1; Hull Tank, 8; Buggelin Tank near Hance Ranch, 1; Moran Point, 1 (GCM); Desert View, 4 (3, GCM; 1, USBS); 1¾ mi. E Desert View Point, 1; SE park boundary, route 64, 1; top Bright Angel Trail [S side?], 6 (USBS).

Eutamias minimus consobrinus (J. A. Allen). NORTH RIM: Tipover Spring, 3;[7] near park entrance, road W-3, 1; ½ mi. S park entrance, 8; The Basin, 10.

Eutamias umbrinus adsitus J. A. Allen. NORTH RIM: "Powell Plateau," 20;[8] Swamp Point, 7,520 ft., 1; Swamp Lake, 7,850 ft., 5; 1 mi. NE Kanabownits Spring, 3; near park entrance, road W-3, 3; 5 mi. N Bright Angel Ranger Station, 1; 5 mi. N, 1 mi. E Bright Angel Ranger Station, 4; The Basin, 5; Thompson Canyon, ½ mi. N Bright Angel Ranger Station, 4; Fuller Canyon, road E-2, 3; Fuller Canyon, road W-2, 1; Neal Spring, 3; ½ mi. S Neal Spring, 2; Point Imperial, 8,800 ft., 5; Greenland Lake, Walhalla Plateau, 1.

Sciurus aberti aberti Woodhouse. SOUTH RIM: Grand Canyon Village, 27 (GCM); 3 mi. S Grand Canyon Village, 1 (GCM); Yavapai Point, 4 (USBS); between Yavapai and Yaki points, 1 (GCM); Grapevine Canyon, 1 (GCM); 2 mi. W Grandview Point, 1 (GCM); 1 mi. W Grandview Point, 2 (GCM); Grandview, 9 (2, UI; 6, GCM; 1, USBS); Hull Tank, 1; 1 mi. W Buggelin

[6] Durham, "Rodents of the North Rim," p. 238.

[7] *Ibid.*, p. 237.

[8] *Ibid.*, p. 238.

Tank, 1; Buggelin Hill, 1 (GCM); 10 mi. E Grand Canyon (Village), 7,500 ft., 1 (Museum of Vertebrate Zoology).

Sciurus kaibabensis Merriam. NORTH RIM: 3½ mi. S Kanabownits Spring, 1; Point Sublime, 1 (GCM); head Kaibab Trail, 1 (GCM); head Bright Angel Creek, 2 (USBS); Bright Angel Spring, 6 (USBS); public campground, 1 (GCM); "near Dormitory," 1 (GCM); Bright Angel Point, 2 (GCM); Farview, 1 (GCM); main highway, 1 (GCM); "cabin 199," 1 (GCM).

Tamiasciurus hudsonicus mogollonensis (Mearns). NORTH RIM: Swamp Lake, 7,850 ft., 2; Tipover Spring, 8,200 ft., 1 (GCM); 4 mi. NE Kanabownits Spring, 1; 4 mi. NW Kanabownits Spring, 1; Point Sublime, 1 (GCM); Fawn Springs, 3; near North Rim entrance, road W-3, 4; ½ mi. S North Rim entrance, 1; Lindberg Hill Highway, 1 (GCM); near mill site, Robbers Roost Ridge, 8,200 ft., 1 (GCM); The Basin, 2; Marble Flats, 1 (GCM); campgrounds, 1 (GCM); Bright Angel Point, 1 (GCM); Fuller Canyon, road E-2, 7; Fuller Canyon, road W-2, 6; 4 mi. NE Neal Spring, 1; ½ mi. S Neal Spring, 1; Point Imperial, 1 (GCM); Farview, 1 (GCM); Cape Royal Highway, 1 (GCM).

Thomomys bottae fulvus (Woodhouse). SOUTH RIM: Pasture Wash, junction of roads W-9 and W-9A, 5; ½ mi. N Pasture Wash Ranger Station, 1; Pasture Wash, 6,300 ft., 2 (1, GCM); 2 mi. S Pasture Wash Ranger Station, 1; Hermit Basin, 1; ¾ mi. SW Rowes Well, 1; ¼ mi. S The Abyss, 4; Grand Canyon Village (school athletic field), 21; Yavapai Point, 1 (GCM); Long Jim Canyon, 21; 2½ mi. W, ½ mi. S Grandview Point, 4; Hearst Ranch, Grandview, 4; 1 mi. SE Grandview, 1; Hull Tank, 4; Buggelin Ranch Tank, 3; 1¼ mi. E Desert View Point, 1; SE park boundary, route 64, 9; N side Cedar Mountain, 1; E side Cedar Mountain, 6,400 ft., 2.

Thomomys bottae boreorarius Durham. NORTH RIM: Powell Spring, 6,200 ft., 2 (GCM); Muav Saddle, 6,700-7,000 ft., 7 (2, GCM); corral near Muav Trail, Powell Plateau, 7,650 ft., 1 (GCM); Swamp Point, 7,523 ft., 2 (GCM); Swamp Lake, 1.

Thomomys talpoides kaibabensis Goldman. NORTH RIM: Swamp Lake, 7,700 ft., 1 (GCM); Tipover Spring, 8,200 ft., 4 (GCM);

Kanabownits Spring, 3; Point Sublime Road near Coffee Lake, 8,500 ft., 3 (GCM); Fawn Springs, 9; near north entrance, road W-3, 7; Robbers Roost Spring, 8,700 ft., 3 (GCM); 5 mi. N, 1 mi. E Bright Angel Ranger Station, 11; The Basin, 17; Marble Flats, 5 (GCM); Harvey Camp, 8,300 ft., 2; Bright Angel Point, 1 (GCM); Thompson Canyon, 1/2 mi. N Bright Angel Ranger Station, 1; Fuller Canyon, road E-2, 14; Greenland Lake, Walhalla Plateau, 6; Snowshoe Cabin, 8,400 ft., 3 (GCM).

Perognathus flavus bimaculatus Merriam. SOUTH RIM: Pasture Wash Ranger Station, 6,300 ft., 1.

Perognathus flavus hopiensis Goldman. SOUTH RIM: SE park boundary, route 64, 1; W side Cedar Mountain, 6,400 ft., 6,550 ft., 2; E side Cedar Mountain, 6,400 ft., 1.

Perognathus intermedius crinitus Benson. SOUTH RIM: Supai Canyon, 5 (USBS); 1/4 mi. upriver from mouth Kanab Creek, S shore, 1 (S. F. State); Hilltop, 5,415 ft., 17; 6 mi. N Bass Camp, 23 (USBS); 1 mi. N Bass Camp, 5,200 ft., 1 (USBS); Elves Chasm, Mile 116.5, 2,100 ft., 4 (MNA); mouth Hermit Creek, Mile 95, 2,500 ft., 2 (MNA); Indian Garden, 3,800 ft., 23 (2, USBS); S Indian Garden, 4,000 ft., 2; below Indian Garden, 1/2 to 2 mi. by trail, 17; Garden Creek, 1 1/2 mi. below Indian Garden, 1 (GCM); Pipe Creek, 2,500 ft., 1 (USBS); Hance Rapids, Mile 76.5, 2,608 ft., 3 (BYU/MNA); McCormick Mine, 1 (USBS); Palisades Creek, Mile 66, 2,675 ft., 1 (BYU/MNA).

Perognathus formosus melanocaudus Cockrum. NORTH RIM: Nankoweap Canyon, 3 mi. from Colorado River, 3,600 ft., 1 (MNA); Kwagunt Creek, 2 mi. W Colorado River, 3,200 ft., 1 (MNA); mouth Kwagunt Creek on Colorado River, 2,800 ft., 3 (MNA); Deer Creek Falls, Mile 136, Kaibab National Forest, 1,925 ft., 1 (BYU/MNA).

Dipodomys ordii chapmani Mearns. SOUTH RIM: Pasture Wash Ranger Station, 1; 1 mi. S Pasture Wash Ranger Station, 3; 2 mi. S Pasture Wash Ranger Station, 6,300 ft., 4; [Trash Tank, 2 (USBS)].

Castor canadensis repentinus Goldman. NORTH RIM: Bright Angel Creek near Phantom Ranch, 1 (GCM). For sight records, see text.

Onychomys leucogaster fuliginosus Merriam. SOUTH RIM: Pasture Wash, 4; 1 mi. S Pasture Wash Ranger Station, 1; Hermit Basin, 2; SE park boundary, route 64, 4; W side Cedar Mountain, 5; E side Cedar Mountain, 1; [Trash Tank, 2 (GCM)].

Reithrodontomys megalotis megalotis (Baird). NORTH RIM: Deer Creek Falls, Mile 136, Kaibab National Forest, 1,925 ft., 2 (BYU/MNA); mouth Bright Angel Creek, 2,500 ft., 2; Bright Angel Creek, 3,000 ft., 1 (GCM); Fuller Canyon, road E-2, 1; Cape Royal, 7,750 ft., 2; Nankoweap Canyon, 3 mi. from Colorado River, 3,600 ft., 1 (MNA). SOUTH RIM: ¾ mi. SW Rowes Well, 4; Grand Canyon Village, 1 (GCM); Indian Garden, 3,800 ft., 1 (USBS); Buggelin Tank, 5; SE park boundary, route 64, 8; W side Cedar Mountain, 6,500 ft., 7; E side Cedar Mountain, 6,400 ft., 2.

Peromyscus maniculatus rufinus (Merriam). NORTH RIM: Muav Saddle, 6,700 ft., 4; Swamp Lake, 2; 1 mi. NE Kanabownits Spring, 1; Kanabownits Spring, 5; Point Sublime, 7,450 ft., 5; Coffee Lake, 1 (GCM); Shiva Temple, 24 (AM); head Kaibab Trail, 2; ½ mi. down Kaibab Trail, 3; Fawn Springs, 7; near entrance, road W-3, 8; ½ mi. S north entrance, 6; Robbers Roost, 9,000 ft., 1 (GCM); 5 mi. N, 1 mi. E Bright Angel Ranger Station, 6; Marble Flats, 1 (GCM); North Rim administration building, 1; Fuller Canyon, road E-2, 7; Fuller Canyon, road W-2, 3; Neal Spring, 3; Point Imperial, 8,800 ft., 19; Greenland Lake, 15; Snowshoe Cabin, 8,400 ft., 2 (GCM); Cape Final, 7,900 ft., 11; Cape Royal, 7,750 ft., 6; Bright Angel Ranger Station, 9; Kwagunt delta on Colorado River, 2,800 ft., 1 (MNA); Nankoweap Campground, Mile 53, 2,775 ft., 6 (5, BYU/MNA; 1, S. F. State). SOUTH RIM: 1 mi. N Bass Camp, 5,200 ft., 1 (USBS); Bass Camp, 3 (USBS); 3 mi. S Bass Camp, 6,400 ft., 3 (USBS); Pasture Wash Ranger Station, 6,300 ft., 23; S park boundary, 1 mi. S Pasture Wash Ranger Station, 2; Hermits Rest, 3; Hermit Basin, 9; Rowes Well, 16; ¾ mi. SW Rowes Well, 21; Grand Canyon Village, 40; Indian Garden, 1; 1¾ mi. down trail from Indian Garden, 1; 2 mi. down trail from Indian Garden, 1; Shoshone Point, 1; Long Jim Canyon, 27; 2 mi. W, ½ mi. S Grandview Point, 17; Grandview Point, 12; Hearst Ranch, Grandview, 8; Hearst Ranch Tank, 6; Hull Tank, 18; Buggelin Tank (Ranch), 18;

Desert View Point, 3; SE park boundary, route 64, 39; W side Cedar Mountain, 15; E side Cedar Mountain, 9; Palisades Creek, Mile 66, 2,675 ft., 3 (BYU/MNA).

Peromyscus boylii rowleyi (J. A. Allen). NORTH RIM: Muav Saddle, 6,700 ft., 6; Deer Creek Falls, Mile 136, Kaibab National Forest, 1,925 ft., 1 (BYU/MNA); Point Sublime, 7,450 ft., 4; Shiva Temple, 3 (AM); mouth Bright Angel Creek, 2,300 ft., 2 (USBS); Phantom Ranch, 1 (USBS); head Kaibab Trail, 2; ½ mi. down Kaibab Trail, 7; Cape Final, 7,900 ft., 6; Cape Royal, 7,750 ft., 1; Nankoweap Valley, 3 mi. above Colorado River, 23 (22, MNA; 1, GCM); Kwagunt Creek, 2 mi. W Colorado River, 3,200 ft., 6 (MNA); Kwagunt delta on Colorado River, 2,800 ft., 2 (MNA). SOUTH RIM: Hilltop, 5,415 ft., 6; top rim near Village, 6,800 ft., 2 (USBS); Indian Garden, 3,800 ft., 12 (8, GCM; 2, USBS; 2, UI); 1½ mi. below Indian Garden, 1 (GCM); up trail from Indian Garden, 4,000 ft., 1; Shoshone Point, 5; Long Jim Canyon, 4; Grandview Point, 10; Grandview Trail, 7,150 ft., 3; Hull Tank, 1; Moran Point, 7,150 ft., 1; ¼ mi. SE Desert View, 1 (GCM); 1 mi. E, ½ mi. S Desert View Point, 4; SE park boundary, route 64, 1; E side Cedar Mountain, 2.

Peromyscus truei truei (Shufeldt). NORTH RIM: Point Sublime, 7,450 ft., 4; Shiva Temple, 12 (1, GCM; 11, AM); Point Imperial, 8,800 ft., 1; Cape Royal, 7,750 ft., 6. SOUTH RIM: Hilltop, 5,415 ft., 4; Pasture Wash, junction of roads W-9A and W-9, 6,900 ft., 2; Hermits Rest, 2; Hermit Basin, 4; Grand Canyon Village, 5 (3, GCM); Shoshone Point, 4; Grandview Point, 2; W side Zuni Point, 7,200 ft., 15; Desert View, 1 (GCM); ¼ mi. S Desert View, 1 (GCM); 1 mi. E, ½ mi. S Desert View Point, 1; SE park boundary, route 64, 19; W side Cedar Mountain, 6,550 ft., 1; E side Cedar Mountain, 6,400 ft., 14.

Peromyscus crinitus auripectus (Allen). NORTH RIM: Mile 156, N side Colorado River, 1,800 ft., 4 (MNA); mouth Kanab Creek, Kaibab National Forest, 1,900 ft., 2 (MNA); mouth Fishtail Canyon, Mile 139, Kaibab National Forest, 1,950 ft., 2 (MNA); mouth Tapeats Creek, Mile 134, 2,000 ft., 3 (MNA); Mile 128, 2,100 ft., 6 (MNA); Hotauta Canyon, Mile 108, 2,266 ft., 7 (BYU/MNA);

just upriver from Bass Camp on E shore Colorado River, 1 (S. F. State); mouth Crystal Creek, Mile 99, 2 (MNA); Point Sublime, 7,450 ft., 5; Shinumo Creek, 3,000 ft., 12 (USBS); Shiva Temple, 4 (AM); mouth Bright Angel Creek, 2,500 ft., 9; Bright Angel Creek, 1 (GCM); Phantom Ranch, 12 (USBS); Point Imperial, 8,800 ft., 1; Cape Royal, 2; Point Honan, 7,950 ft., 1;[9] Nankoweap Valley, 3 mi. above Colorado River, 14 (1, GCM; 13, MNA); Nankoweap Campground, Mile 53, 2,775 ft., 2 (BYU/MNA); Kwagunt Creek, 2 mi. W Colorado River, 3,200 ft., 4 (MNA); mouth Kwagunt Creek Canyon on Colorado River, 2,800 ft., 7 (MNA); Chuar Creek, 1 (USBS). SOUTH RIM: Supai Canyon, 1 (USBS); 6 mi. N [by trail?] Bass Camp, 2 (USBS); 1 mi. N [by trail?] Bass Camp, 1 (USBS); mouth Hermit Creek, Mile 95, 2,500 ft., 1 (MNA); Yavapai Point Trail, 1 (USBS); Pipe Creek, 1 (USBS).

Peromyscus eremicus eremicus (Baird). NORTH RIM: mouth Kanab Creek, Mile 143.5, Kaibab National Forest, 1,900 ft., 2 (MNA); mouth Fishtail Canyon, Mile 139, Kaibab National Forest, 1,950 ft., 1 (MNA); Deer Creek Falls, Mile 136, Kaibab National Forest, 1,925 ft., 5 (BYU/MNA); mouth Tapeats Creek, Mile 134, 2,000 ft., 2 (MNA); Hotauta Canyon, Mile 108, 2,266 ft., 3 (BYU/MNA); mouth Crystal Creek, Mile 99, 3 (MNA); Shinumo Creek, 3,000 ft., 22 (USBS); mouth Bright Angel Creek, 2,500 ft., 11 (1, GCM); Phantom Ranch, 10 (USBS); Bright Angel Point, 8,153 ft., 1 (GCM); Nankoweap Canyon, 3 mi. from Colorado River, 3,600 ft., 4 (MNA); Nankoweap Campground, Mile 53, 2,775 ft., 5 (BYU/ MNA); Kwagunt Creek, 2 mi. W Colorado River, 1 (MNA); mouth Kwagunt Creek on Colorado River, 2,800 ft., 6 (MNA); Chuar Creek, 3 (USBS). SOUTH RIM: Supai Canyon, 4 (USBS); Hilltop, 5,415 ft., 1; 100 yds. upstream from mouth Kanab Creek, 1 (S. F. State); Elves Chasm, Mile 116.5, 2,100 ft., 4 (MNA); 6 mi. N [by trail] Bass Camp, 3,400 ft., 6 (USBS); 1 mi. N Bass Camp, 5,200 ft., 4 (USBS); Bass Camp, 3,500 ft., 3 (USBS); mouth Hermit Creek, Mile 95, 2,500 ft., 2 (MNA); Indian Garden, 23; along Bright Angel Trail, ½ mi. below Indian Garden, 5; 1⅖ mi. below, 6; Tonto Plateau below Indian Garden, 10; 1 mi. below, 2; 1¾ mi. below, 4; 2 mi.

[9] *Ibid.*, p. 244.

below, 2; up Bright Angel Trail from Indian Garden, 4,000 ft., 2; Pipe Creek, 2,500 ft., 3 (USBS); Hance Rapids, Mile 76.5, 2,608 ft., 11 (BYU/MNA); Mile 70, 2,700 ft., 4 (MNA); Colorado River at foot Tanner Trail, 3 (GCM); McCormick Mine, 2 (GCM); Palisades Creek, Mile 66, 2,675 ft., 7 (MNA); opposite Lava Canyon, 1 (S. F. State); junction of Little Colorado River, Mile 61.5, 2,800 ft., 5 (MNA); on Little Colorado River, 1½ mi. E junction with Colorado River, 4 (MNA).

Neotoma lepida monstrabilis Goldman. NORTH RIM: mouth Tapeats Creek, Mile 134, 2,000 ft., 2 (1, MNA; 1, S. F. State); Muav Saddle, 6,700 ft., 1; Point Sublime, 3; Shinumo Creek, 3,000 ft., 2 (USBS); Hotauta Canyon, Mile 108, 2,266 ft., 2 (BYU/MNA); mouth Bright Angel Creek, 2,500 ft., 3; Phantom Ranch, 3 (USBS); Bright Angel Canyon below Ribbon Falls, 1 (GCM); Bright Angel Creek, 1 (GCM); Point Imperial, 8,800 ft., 2; Nankoweap Canyon, 1 (GCM); Nankoweap Canyon, 3 mi. from Colorado River, 3,600 ft., 3 (MNA); Kwagunt delta on Colorado River, 2,800 ft., 1 (MNA).

Neotoma lepida devia Goldman. SOUTH RIM: across from mouth Kanab Canyon, 1 (S. F. State); 6 mi. N Bass Camp, 16 (USBS); Bright Angel Trail, 1.6 mi. below Indian Garden, 1; Indian Garden, 2 (USBS); Pipe Creek, 2,500 ft., 1 (USBS); McCormick Mine, 2 (USBS).

Neotoma stephensi stephensi Goldman. SOUTH RIM: Hilltop, 5,415 ft., 4; 1 mi. N Bass Camp, 5,200 ft., 2 (USBS); Bass Camp, 1 (USBS); 3 mi. S Bass Camp, 6,400 ft., 3 (USBS); Pasture Wash, junction of roads W-9A and W-9, 1; Pasture Wash Ranger Station, 6,300 ft., 3; near Rowes Well, 1; Grand Canyon Village, 8 (1, GCM; 1, USBS; 6, UI); Yavapai Point, 3 (GCM); Yaki Point, 2 (USBS); Yaki Burn, 2 (GCM); Shoshone Point, 2; Long Jim Canyon, 3; Grandview Point, 2 (1, USBS); W side Zuni Point, 7,200 ft., 6; Wayside Museum, 1 (GCM); 1 mi. E, ½ mi. S Desert View Point, 1; SE park boundary, route 64, 1; E side Cedar Mountain, 6,400 ft., 2.

Neotoma albigula laplataensis Miller. SOUTH RIM: Supai Canyon, 1 (USBS); Hilltop, 5,415 ft., 3; 1 mi. N Bass Camp, 2 (USBS); Bass Camp, 5; mouth Hermit Creek, Mile 95, 2,500 ft., 1 (MNA);

Pasture Wash, junction of roads W-9 and W-9A, 3; Grand Canyon Village, 2 (GCM); Indian Garden, 2 (GCM); Tonto Plateau, 1 mi. by trail below Indian Garden, 2; Garden Creek, 1½ mi. below Indian Garden, 1 (GCM); Grandview Point, 1 (USBS); Desert View, 1 (GCM); Colorado River at foot Tanner Trail, 1 (GCM); W side Cedar Mountain, 1; N side Cedar Mountain, 6,500 ft., 1; E side Cedar Mountain, 6,400 ft., 8; Mile 70, 2,700 ft., 2 (MNA); Palisades Creek, Mile 66, 2,675 ft., 1 (BYU/MNA).

Neotoma mexicana pinetorum Merriam. SOUTH RIM: Bass Camp, 6,600 ft., 4 (USBS); near Village at top of rim and just under rim, 6,500-6,800 ft., 5 (USBS); Indian Garden, 3,800 ft., 9 (1, GCM; 8, USBS); Yavapai Point, under rim, 1 (USBS); Long Jim Canyon, 4; 2 mi. W, ½ mi. S Grandview Point, 4; Grandview Point, 1; Hearst Ranch, Grandview, 5.

Neotoma cinerea acraia (Elliot). NORTH RIM: Shiva Temple, 4 (AM); head Kaibab Trail, 1; Marble Flats, 1 (GCM); North Rim Ranger Station, 4 (GCM); Bright Angel Point, 4 (GCM); mule barn near headquarters, 2 (GCM); Point Imperial, 8,800 ft., 7 (2, GCM); Point Honan, 1.[10]

Microtus longicaudus baileyi (Goldman). NORTH RIM: Swamp Lake, 2; Tipover Spring, 8,200 ft., 1 (GCM); 1 mi. NE Kanabownits Spring, 1; Kanabownits Spring, 4; Fawn Springs, 8; near park entrance, road W-3, 3; ½ mi. S park entrance, 2; Robbers Roost, 9,000 ft., 1 (GCM); Robbers Roost Spring, 8,700 ft., 1 (GCM); 5 mi. N, 1 mi. E Bright Angel Ranger Station, 20; The Basin, 20; Marble Flats, 2 (GCM); Fuller Canyon, 11; Fuller Canyon, road E-2, 12; Fuller Spring, 1 (GCM); Neal Spring, 12; campground near Neal Spring, 1; Point Imperial, 8,800 ft., 1; Greenland Lake, 7; Snowshoe Cabin, 8,400 ft., Walhalla Plateau, 4 (GCM).

Microtus mexicanus mogollonensis (Mearns). SOUTH RIM: 3 mi. S Bass Camp, 6,400 ft., 19 (USBS); Pasture Wash, junction of roads W-9A and W-9, 5; Pasture Wash Ranger Station, 6,300 ft., 6; ¾ mi. SW Rowes Well, 9; Grand Canyon Village, 8 (2, GCM); head Bright Angel Trail, 1 (GCM); Indian Garden, 2; Long Jim Canyon,

[10] *Ibid.*, p. 247.

45; 2 mi. W, ½ mi. S Grandview Point, 5; Hearst Ranch Tank, Grandview, 9; Hull Tank, 21; Buggelin Tank near Hance Ranch, 24; SE park boundary, route 64, 4; W side Cedar Mountain, 6,550 ft., 1.

Mus musculus (subspecies). SOUTH RIM: Grand Canyon Village, 4 (GCM).

Erethizon dorsatum epixanthum Brandt. NORTH RIM: near park entrance, road W-3, 1. Sight records: Point Sublime Road, Long Road in Thompson Canyon, Shiva Temple, Bright Angel Point, Grand Canyon Lodge.

Erethizon dorsatum couesi Mearns. SOUTH RIM: S park boundary, 1 mi. S Pasture Wash Ranger Station, 1; Grand Canyon Village, 1 (GCM); Wayside Museum, 1 (GCM); Desert View, 1 (GCM). Sight records: Mesa Eremita, Abyss, near Hermits Rest, Mohave Point, Powell Memorial, Yavapai Point, Yaki Point, Grandview, Buggelin Hill, Moran Point.

Odocoileus hemionus hemionus (Rafinesque). NORTH RIM: Point Imperial Road, 1 (USBS). Sight records: Shiva Temple, on top of rim from Powell Plateau and Swamp Point to Cape Final, mouth Bright Angel Creek, Phantom Ranch, Imperial Road, along Nankoweap Creek, Chuar Creek. SOUTH RIM: Sight records: Pasture Wash to near Desert View, along Bright Angel Trail, Indian Garden, on Tonto Plateau at various places, as near Pipe Creek.

Antilocapra americana (americana?). SOUTH RIM: none examined (see account for records).

Ovis canadensis mexicana Merriam. SOUTH RIM: mouth Cataract [actually Havasu] Canyon, 8 (USBS); Desert View, 1 (USBS). NORTH RIM: see records in text.

INDEX